Science
Worksheets
Don't Grow Dendrites

Science Worksheets

Don't Grow Dendrites

20
Instructional
Strategies
That Engage
the Brain

Marcia L. Tate
Warren G. Phillips

CORWIN
A SAGE Company

Illustrations by Robert Greisen.

For information:

Corwin
A SAGE Company
2455 Teller Road
Thousand Oaks, California 91320
www.corwin.com

SAGE Ltd.
1 Oliver's Yard
55 City Road
London EC1Y 1SP
United Kingdom

SAGE Pvt. Ltd.
B 1/I 1 Mohan Cooperative
   Industrial Area
Mathura Road, New Delhi 110 044
India

SAGE Asia-Pacific Pte. Ltd.
33 Pekin Street #02-01
Far East Square
Singapore 048763

Printed in the United States of America

Library of Congress Cataloging-in-Publication Data

Tate, Marcia L.
Science worksheets don't grow dendrites : 20 instructional strategies that engage the brain / Marcia L. Tate and Warren G. Phillips.
     p. cm.
Includes bibliographical references and index.
ISBN 978-1-4129-7847-7 (pbk. : alk. paper)
   1. Cognitive neuroscience. 2. Learning, Psychology of. 3. Brain. I. Phillips, Warren G. II. Title. III. Title: Twenty strategies that engage the brain.

QP360.5.T37 2011
612.8'233—dc22   2010026677

This book is printed on acid-free paper.

10 11 12 13 14 10 9 8 7 6 5 4 3 2 1

Acquisitions Editor:	Carol Chambers Collins
Associate Editor:	Megan Bedell
Editorial Assistant:	Sarah Bartlett
Production Editor:	Veronica Stapleton
Copy Editor:	Cynthia Long
Typesetter:	C&M Digitals (P) Ltd.
Proofreader:	Cheryl Rivard
Indexer:	Molly Hall
Cover Designer:	Rose Storey

The authors have made every reasonable effort to ensure that the experiments and activities described in this book and on its companion website www.corwin.com/scienceworksheets are safe when conducted as instructed but assume no responsibility for any damage caused or sustained while performing said experiments or activities.

All information and materials supplied are viewed and interpreted solely at your own risk. The authors do not intend to explain all dangers known or unknown that may result from the building or operation of any project. All content is presented solely for educational and entertainment purposes. Parents, guardians, and teachers should supervise young readers who undertake the experiments and activities described.

Contents

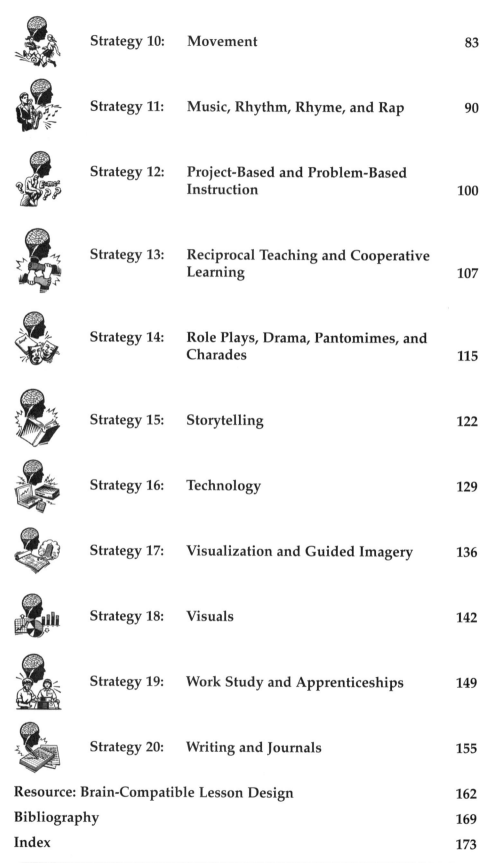

Additional materials and resources related to *Science Worksheets Don't Grow Dendrites: 20 Strategies That Engage the Brain* can be found at www.corwin.com/scienceworksheets

Acknowledgments

My very favorite quote when it comes to teaching is the following:

> *Teachers are those who use themselves as bridges over which they invite their students to cross, and then, having facilitated their crossing, joyfully collapse, inviting their students to build bridges of their own.*
>
> —Nikos Kazantzakis

More than 10 years ago, I had the privilege of meeting one such "bridge builder." His name is Warren Phillips, and at the time that he sat in the workshop I was conducting, he was teaching science at a middle school in Plymouth, Massachusetts. Over the years, I have learned more from Warren Phillips about effective teaching and learning, particularly in the area of science, than he ever learned from me. This is why I elicited his help in writing this book. I am a reading specialist, and while I know how content needs to be delivered, I do not possess the extensive content knowledge essential for getting students so turned on to science that many of them go on to Ivy League universities and major in science. Warren Phillips does! He was the 2004 Disney Outstanding Middle School Teacher of the Year; and in 2006, *USA Today* named Warren as one of the 25 top teachers in the United States.

I owe Warren a great debt of gratitude for agreeing to provide many of the sample classroom activities that you will read about in this book. He knows that these lessons work since he has actually used them with his students in his class. I acknowledge him and the other teachers like him who get students so excited about learning that they pursue a lifelong love of the content.

Here is a true story that is quite coincidental. My nephew, Gerald, married a lady from Plymouth, Massachusetts, by the name of Kim. In fact, I was present at their wedding. One day during a family gathering, the conversation turned to education. Kim casually mentioned that there had been one teacher in her educational career that she would never forget. She related that he had made science so much fun that she looked forward to going to class every day. She began to tell us all of the concepts that she still remembered because of the way she was taught in this class. Guess who her teacher was? You're right, Warren Phillips. Thank you, Warren, for your contributions to this book and, more important, to the lives of countless students and their families. Your impact will be felt for generations to come!

■ PUBLISHER'S ACKNOWLEDGMENTS

Corwin gratefully acknowledges the contributions of the following reviewers:

Dana Aguilera, Assistant Principal and Science Coordinator
Las Palmas Elementary School, San Clemente, California

D. Allan Bruner, Science Chair and Teacher
Colton High School, Colton, Oregon

Gina Hickerson, District Science Leader
Centralia Elementary School District, Buena Park, California

Emily Neddersen, Lead Science Teacher
Myford Elementary School, Tustin, California

Kathi Wagner, English Learner/Categorical Program Coordinator
Centralia School District, Buena Park, California

About the Authors

 **Marcia L. Tate, EdD,** is the former executive director of professional development for the DeKalb County School System, Decatur, Georgia. During her 30-year career with the district, she has been a classroom teacher, reading specialist, language arts coordinator, and staff development executive director. She received the Distinguished Staff Developer Award for the state of Georgia, and her department was chosen to receive the Exemplary Program Award for the state.

Marcia is currently an educational consultant and has taught more than 300,000 administrators, teachers, parents, and business and community leaders throughout the world, including Australia, Egypt, Hungary, Singapore, and New Zealand. She is the author of the following five best sellers: *Worksheets Don't Grow Dendrites: 20 Instructional Strategies That Engage the Brain; "Sit & Get" Won't Grow Dendrites: 20 Professional Learning Strategies That Engage the Adult Brain; Reading and Language Arts Worksheets Don't Grow Dendrites: 20 Literacy Strategies That Engage the Brain; Shouting Won't Grow Dendrites: 20 Techniques for Managing a Brain-Compatible Classroom;* and *Mathematics Worksheets Don't Grow Dendrites: 20 Numeracy Strategies That Engage the Brain.* Participants in her workshops refer to them as "some of the best ones they have ever experienced" since Marcia uses the 20 strategies outlined in her books to actively engage her audiences.

Marcia received her bachelor's degree in psychology and elementary education from Spelman College in Atlanta, Georgia. She earned her master's degree in remedial reading from the University of Michigan, her specialist degree in educational leadership from Georgia State University, and her doctorate in educational leadership from Clark Atlanta University. Spelman College awarded her the Apple Award for excellence in the field of education.

Marcia is married to Tyrone Tate and is the proud mother of three children, Jennifer, Jessica, and Christopher; and the doting grandmother of two granddaughters, Christian and Aidan. Marcia can be contacted by calling her company at (770) 918-5039 or by e-mail at marciata@bellsouth.net. Visit her website at www.developingmindsinc.com.

Warren G. Phillips, MEd, has been married for 34 years to his high school sweetheart, Karen. They have two children: Jeffrey, who recently earned a doctorate in family medicine, and Kristin, a student with learning challenges and also an advocate for students with learning challenges, who works at Cape Cod Community College. Warren's hobbies include music (keyboard and guitar), woodworking, and gardening.

Mr. Phillips was a seventh-grade science teacher in Plymouth, Massachusetts, where he's taught for 35 years. He created a service-learning course for seventh graders called HOWL (Helping Others While Learning) and maintains an informative website at www.wphillips.com. Warren's HOWL students initiated a recycling program, classroom lessons, school activities, and many video productions for the local cable channel. He has a BA in earth sciences, an MAT in teaching physical sciences, and an MEd in instructional technology from Bridgewater State College in Bridgewater, Massachusetts.

Warren is a contributing writer for the Prentice Hall *Science Explorer* series and has written curriculum for Northeastern University's Project SEED (science education through experiments and demonstrations) and the Plymouth Public Schools science curriculum. He's also a certified teacher for the National Board for Professional Teaching Standards (NBPTS). He was chosen Teacher of the Year in Time for Kids Chevrolet Teaching Excellence Award contest in 2002, winning a Chevy Malibu and $2,000 for his classroom. He won the Massachusetts Software and Internet Council's Above and Beyond Award in 2002 and 2003. Warren recorded and produced a series of three CDs of science songs titled *Sing-A-Long Science.*

In 2004, he was selected for a DisneyHand Teaching Award honoring creativity in teaching. From the 39 DisneyHand teachers, he was selected as Middle School Teacher of the Year, an honor he treasures. His award-winning teaching performance earned him a guest appearance on the *Tony Danza Show*. In 2005, Warren was selected as a contestant on *Who Wants to Be a Millionaire*. His essay about teaching is featured in the NSTA (National Science Teachers Association) monograph titled *Exemplary Science in Grades 5–8: Standards-Based Success Stories* (Yager, 2006). In 2006, he was named as a member of the USA Today All-USA Teaching Team.

Warren was selected as the Massachusetts Science Teacher of the Year for Plymouth County in 2006 and also earned the Presidential Volunteer Service Award. He appeared in a commercial for Bridgewater State College. In June of 2008, Warren went to Kenya to study elephants on an Earthwatch Research Fellowship. He was recently inducted into the Massachusetts Science Educators Hall of Fame. He is a contributing author in an uplifting book about teaching called *Today, I Made a Difference* (Underwood, 2009). He has initiated a grant program and created a teaching award for exemplary Plymouth teachers through a local foundation called Science Technology Educational Partnership (STEP). In June 2010, Warren was one of five teachers to be inducted into the National Teachers Hall of Fame in Emporia, Kansas.

Introduction

Learning can and often does take place without the benefit of teaching—and sometimes even in spite of it—but there is no such thing as effective teaching in the absence of learning.

—Angelo and Cross (1993, p. 3)

Speaking of learning in spite of, or because of, visualize the two science classrooms as you read the following scenarios. Ask yourself these questions: *How are these two classrooms alike? How are they different? Which science teacher would you rather have had when you were a middle school student? Which teacher epitomizes the way most teachers teach science today?*

■ SCENARIO I

Mr. McIntire teaches science at Pine Lake Middle School. Let's look in on his class. Some of Mr. McIntire's seventh graders are filing into his classroom. Others are standing outside in the hall talking and, after being asked repeatedly, slowly saunter into the classroom. Once the second bell rings, Mr. McIntire checks roll by calling the names of every student in class and listening for the response of *here* or *present*. This goes on for some time, and since students are bored, they begin talking to peers in close proximity, for which they are promptly reprimanded. Six minutes later, class begins with a review of the homework from the night before. Students were assigned to write the answers to all of the questions at the end of the textbook chapter covered on yesterday. Many students come in without their homework, so they have nothing to look at while the remainder of the class listens to Mr. McIntire give the answers orally. Students mark their answers as correct or incorrect. Finally, after about 20 minutes, the lesson for the day begins. The objective addresses the Physical Science Content Standard *properties and changes of properties in matter*. Students are told to open their textbooks to Chapter 5, Section 1, and the lesson begins. Students will be taking turns reading the chapter aloud while the remainder of the class follows along. Mr. McIntire stops periodically to ask questions of volunteers. Nonvolunteers are never called upon, and some tune out completely. This goes on for the remainder of the period. The homework assignment tonight will be to answer the questions at the end of Chapter 5, Section 1, for discussion tomorrow. Since there are a few minutes remaining in class, students are told to begin their homework now and work until the bell rings. When the bell rings, students jump up and run for the door.

■ SCENARIO II

Mrs. Miller teaches middle school science at Douglas Middle School. Students cannot wait to get to her class since they are never quite sure what novel things will be happening each day. They have nicknamed her *Mrs. Science* and she wears the label well! As students come into class, they automatically know to look for a *sponge activity* on the board. Today the activity asks them to continue work in their cooperative groups on the science projects that they began earlier in the week. Students know exactly how to proceed in their groups since they have worked cooperatively all year. The *materials manager* gathers the supplies and each group's *facilitator* leads a group discussion of the progress on the project while Mrs. Miller checks roll quickly using a seating chart. She then takes turns visiting each group for a progress report of their respective projects.

After about 15 minutes of group activity, Mrs. Miller asks that students put up their materials and get ready for today's lesson, which is on the Physical Science Content Standard *properties and changes of properties in matter.* She begins by drawing a K-N-L chart on the board regarding the four states of matter and has students brainstorm what they already *know* and what they think they will *need* to know. Later, they will summarize by filling in the column on what they have *learned.* She finds that both volunteers and nonvolunteers already know a great deal about the topic.

To reinforce the learning, Mrs. Miller then has students stand up and she demonstrates how to simulate atom movement by having them shake their fists. This is a metaphor for the fact that atoms vibrate and have energy. Then students shake two fists to represent two atoms. If the fists are maintaining relative position, she tells them that they are simulating a solid. If the fists rotate around one another, they simulate a liquid. A gas is made by taking the fists and extending them out far away from each other. Plasma is simulated when students are moving their arms wildly and opening their fists to extend fingers, implying that light is released. Tomorrow, students will use these movements in conjunction with the song "The States of Matter," written by Warren Phillips and found on his website at www.wphillips.com. The homework assignment tonight is to find things in their homes that represent each state of matter and bring the list back tomorrow. The bell rings and students reluctantly file out of class. However, several gather around and are engaged in friendly conversations with Mrs. Miller on their way out of the room.

BRAIN-COMPATIBLE INSTRUCTION ◼

I am often asked to conduct model lessons in schools around the world. I will take a teacher's class and teach them while other teachers observe the lesson. Following are two letters from students in a second-grade class that I taught some years ago. I taught a science lesson on the planets and their order from the sun. Notice that this lesson was taught before we lost Pluto as a planet. Once I left, the teacher asked the class to write letters telling me what they had learned, and she mailed those letters to my house. The letters were wonderful, and I share several in my classes when I teach adults. Note that second graders still use invented spelling.

Mrs. Tate tot me my planets in oder. She told us to say My verey educated mother just served us nine pizzas. I know it by heart. We drew the nine planets. I didn't have a nuff roon so I had to write on the side. We listened to music. When she hit the chimes that ment be qiet. We colored planets. I learnt the closest to the sun and the farthest from the sun.

Dear Mrs. Tate,

Thank you! For teaching us about the plants. And how to put them in orber. Also for letting us act it out. I was wonding can you be a teacher one day. You'll be a great teacher. You prodleley teach 2nd gread. Thank you Mrs. Tate for comeing to our school!

Plantes

1. Merkey

2. Vens

3. Earth

4. Mars

5. Jupeter

6. Saturn

7. Uranes

8. Nursen

9. Pluto

This is such an exciting time to be a teacher! While the brain remains a mystery, we know more today than ever about how brains acquire and retain information. The formula is quite simple. Take the research of learning-style theorists (Gardner, 1983; Sternberg & Grigorenko, 2000), combine it with the work of educational consultants (Jensen, E., 2009; Sousa, 2006; Sylwester, 2003), and add a dash of classroom observation regarding the use of best practices. There you have it! The recipe for effective teaching or 20 strategies that take advantage of how all brains learn. These strategies work for elementary, middle school, high school, and college students, as well as adults, in any learning situation. They work for students in special education programs, regular education programs, and gifted programs; students who are learning a second language; and students who have attention deficit disorder. In other words, they work for all students and adults. While these ways are not new—your most effective teachers have used them for generations—what is new is that brain researchers have given us a reason as to why these strategies work better than others. If you really examine the letters from the second graders, you will see that I used at least five of the strategies as I taught them about the planets in order: mnemonic devices, drawing, writing, music, and role play. Whether I am teaching students from kindergarten through 12th grade or adult audiences, I teach absolutely nothing without the 20 strategies. I am challenging you to do the same.

The 20 brain-compatible strategies are as follows:

1. Brainstorming and discussion
2. Drawing and artwork
3. Field trips
4. Games
5. Graphic organizers, semantic maps, and word webs
6. Humor
7. Manipulatives, experiments, labs, and models
8. Metaphors, analogies, and similes
9. Mnemonic devices
10. Movement
11. Music, rhythm, rhyme, and rap
12. Project-based and problem-based instruction
13. Reciprocal teaching and cooperative learning
14. Role plays, drama, pantomimes, and charades
15. Storytelling
16. Technology
17. Visualization and guided imagery
18. Visuals
19. Work study and apprenticeships
20. Writing and journals

By the time teachers have incorporated these strategies into their lessons, they have addressed all of Howard Gardner's (1983) multiple intelligences as well as all four of the major modalities: visual, auditory, kinesthetic, and tactile. Refer to Figure 0.1 for a chart that shows this correlation.

OVERVIEW OF THE NATIONAL SCIENCE EDUCATION STANDARDS ■

The 20 strategies answer the question of how to teach; however, one of the foremost questions any science teacher should be asking is "What am I supposed to teach?" While there are district curricula and state standards, the National Research Council (NRC, 1996) has written a 261-page document called the *National Science Education Standards.* The document is available from the National Academies Press at www.nap.edu/openbook .php?record_id=4962 and contains eight categories of content standards for science. They are as follows:

> Unifying concepts and processes in science
> Science as inquiry
> Physical science
> Life science
> Earth and space science
> Science and technology
> Science in personal and social perspectives
> History and nature of science

These broad categories are further delineated into the grade-level knowledge and skills required to be proficient in the content area of science and should serve as the major *chunks* to be addressed during instruction. This book contains over 250 activities for teaching science in brain-compatible ways. Every activity is correlated to one or more of the grade-level categories that follow:

6.0. Unifying Concepts and Processes Standards

Levels K–12

> Systems, order, and organization
>
> Evidence, models, and explanation
>
> Change, constancy, and measurement
>
> Evolution and equilibrium
>
> Form and function

6.1. Science as Inquiry Standards

Levels K–12

> Abilities necessary to do scientific inquiry
>
> Understanding about scientific inquiry

6.2. Physical Science Standards

Levels K–4

> Properties of objects and materials
>
> Position and motion of objects
>
> Light, heat, electricity, and magnetism

Levels 5–8

> Properties and changes of properties in matter
>
> Motions and forces
>
> Transfer of energy

Levels 9–12

> Structure of atoms
>
> Structure and properties of matter
>
> Chemical reactions
>
> Motions and forces
>
> Conservation of energy and increase in disorder
>
> Interactions of energy and matter

6.3. Life Science Standards

Levels K–4

> Characteristics of organisms
>
> Life cycles of organisms
>
> Organisms and environments

Levels 5–8

> Structure and function in living systems
>
> Reproduction and heredity
>
> Regulation and behavior
>
> Populations and ecosystems
>
> Diversity and adaptations of organisms

Levels 9–12

    The cell

    Molecular basis of heredity

    Biological evolution

    Interdependence of organisms

    Matter, energy, and organization in living systems

    Behavior of organisms

6.4. Earth and Space Science Standards

Levels K–4

    Properties of earth materials

    Objects in the sky

    Changes in earth and sky

Levels 5–8

    Structure of the earth system

    Earth's history

    Earth in the solar system

Levels 9–12

    Energy in the earth system

    Geochemical cycles

    Origin and evolution of the earth system

    Origin and evolution of the universe

6.5. Science and Technology Standards

Levels K–4

    Abilities to distinguish between natural objects and objects made by humans

    Abilities of technological design

    Understanding about science and technology

Levels 5–8

    Abilities of technological design

    Understanding about science and technology

Levels 9–12

> Abilities of technological design
>
> Understanding about science and technology

6.6. Science in Personal and Social Perspectives Standards

Levels K–4

> Personal health
>
> Characteristics and changes in populations
>
> Types of resources
>
> Changes in environments
>
> Science and technology in local challenges

Levels 5–8

> Personal health
>
> Populations, resources, and environments
>
> Natural hazards
>
> Risks and benefits
>
> Science and technology in society

Levels 9–12

> Personal and community health
>
> Population growth
>
> Natural resources
>
> Environmental quality
>
> Natural and human-induced hazards
>
> Science and technology in local, national, and global challenges

6.7. History and Nature of Science Standards

Levels K–4

> Science as a human endeavor

Levels 5–8

> Science as a human endeavor
>
> Nature of science
>
> History of science

Levels 9–12

Science as a human endeavor

Nature of scientific knowledge

Historical perspectives

The remainder of this book provides an explanation of each strategy and more than 200 pieces of research as to why these particular strategies work better than others. It will also provide you with more than 250 activities to incorporate in your lessons to ensure that brain-compatible instruction is taking place. Each activity is correlated to a content standard and a recommended grade level or levels. Many of the activities can be used to address any content standard and at any grade level. A recommendation is also provided as to whether this activity fits best before, during, or after instruction. The advantage of having activities for multiple grade levels in one book is that they can be used as is or adapted for students performing below, on, or above grade level. At the end of each chapter there is a reflection and application page on which you can take your personal curriculum objectives and correlate them to specific activities in the chapter or create original activities based on the strategy.

This book attempts to accomplish the following six major objectives:

1. Introduce you to 20 strategies that take advantage of ways in which the brain learns best

2. Supply over 200 research rationales from experts in the field as to why these strategies work better than others

3. Provide more than 250 activities of how to incorporate the 20 strategies into a K–12 science classroom

4. Correlate the science content standards to each activity

5. Allow time and space at the end of each chapter for the reader to reflect on the application of the strategies as they apply directly to the reader's specific objectives

6. Ask and answer the five questions that every teacher ought to be asking when planning and teaching a brain-compatible science lesson

Enjoy the wide variety of K–12 activities that can make science come alive in your classroom. The most important consideration as you teach science is to take advantage of the natural inclination of human beings to want to solve problems and find answers to questions that present themselves in the real world and to have fun while doing it! Keep these words from our initial quote in mind:

There is no such thing as effective teaching in the absence of learning.

—Angelo and Cross (1993, p. 3)

Comparison of Brain-Compatible Instructional Strategies to Learning Theory		
Brain-Compatible Strategies	*Multiple Intelligences*	*Visual, Auditory, Kinesthetic, Tactile (VAKT)*
Brainstorming and discussion	Verbal-linguistic	Auditory
Drawing and artwork	Spatial	Kinesthetic/tactile
Field trips	Naturalist	Kinesthetic/tactile
Games	Interpersonal	Kinesthetic/tactile
Graphic organizers, semantic maps, and word webs	Logical-mathematical/spatial	Visual/tactile
Humor	Verbal-linguistic	Auditory
Manipulatives, experiments, labs, and models	Logical-mathematical	Tactile
Metaphors, analogies, and similes	Spatial	Visual/auditory
Mnemonic devices	Musical-rhythmic	Visual/auditory
Movement	Bodily-kinesthetic	Kinesthetic
Music, rhythm, rhyme, and rap	Musical-rhythmic	Auditory
Project-based and problem-based instruction	Logical-mathematical	Visual/tactile
Reciprocal teaching and cooperative learning	Verbal-linguistic	Auditory
Role plays, drama, pantomimes, charades	Bodily-kinesthetic	Kinesthetic
Storytelling	Verbal-linguistic	Auditory
Technology	Spatial	Visual/tactile
Visualization and guided imagery	Spatial	Visual
Visuals	Spatial	Visual
Work study and apprenticeships	Interpersonal	Kinesthetic
Writing and journals	Intrapersonal	Visual/tactile

Figure 0.1

Strategy 1

Brainstorming and Discussion

WHAT: DEFINING THE STRATEGY

Which substance has the highest pH value?

Why do finer steel wools burn much longer than thicker ones?

Why will a paper clip float on water?

How do lasers work?

Of all the content areas, science is probably the one that most naturally lends itself to finding answers to relevant questions. When a science teacher arouses the natural curiosity of students' brains through meaningful questioning, discussing the answers to those questions and brainstorming ideas become natural parts of any lesson.

Try the following activity as one that will cause students to think outside the box, much like a scientist. Ask the following question and have students work in cooperative groups to brainstorm as many creative answers as possible: *What is ½ of 8?* The standard answer of the nonscientific mind would be 4. However, consider these responses: Three (3) is the right half of the number (8). The letters *ei* and half of the letter *g* are the left half of the word *eight.* The other half of the letter *g* and the letters *ht* are the right half of the word *eight.* This type of outside-the-box thinking should be encouraged in any classroom but particularly a science one. However, for students to feel comfortable during the process, a variety of ideas should be encouraged and criticism strongly discouraged. After all, the person in the classroom who is doing the most talking about the content is actually growing the most dendrites, or brain cells. Students have got to be let into the conversation.

WHY: THEORETICAL FRAMEWORK

Well-used questioning is a superb way to help students observe and come to understand the ideas and skills that they are learning, while simultaneously absorbing and retaining a great deal of information. (Caine, Caine, McClintic, & Klimek, 2009, p. 209)

The quality and quantity of the questions that real-life scientists ask determines the progress of science in the real world. (Berman, 2008)

During discussion, people can offer data; give their knowledge, ideas, information, and rationales on their positions; and attempt to convince others to see their side. (Costa, 2008)

Questions can be used to promote and show evidence of student thought and play a crucial role in all of the following five phases of instruction: engage, explore, explain, elaborate, and evaluate. (Hammerman, 2009)

When graphic organizers are used in cooperation with group discussion or brainstorming activities, all students are encouraged to contribute. (Jensen, E., 2004)

With appropriate questioning strategies, students can have their minds engaged and transformed. Learners are presented with problems and questions where the answers are not necessarily apparent. (Costa, 2008)

In effective classrooms, the teacher's questioning and guidance encourages students to do most of the talking and doing. (Breaux & Whitaker, 2006)

Having students stop for constructive discussion breaks, even as short as 30 seconds, is not a waste of time but makes class time more productive. (Jensen, R., 2008)

Asking students to discuss with one another any questions about what the teacher has just explained, forces them to verbalize what has been covered and what is not clear. When actual questions come up, they are more concise and articulate. (Jensen, R., 2008)

When students develop their own questions that go beyond the recall level, they must practice metacognition and recognize the level or understanding needed to both ask and answer the question. (Keeley, 2008)

HOW: INSTRUCTIONAL ACTIVITIES

WHEN: Before a lesson

CONTENT STANDARD(S):   Systems, order, and organization (K–12); Structure and function in living systems (5–8)

- To prepare students for the concept of classification, ask them to place one shoe in one corner of the room and the other shoe in another corner. Put students in two groups. Have each group brainstorm as many ways to classify the shoes in one pile as they can think of in 20 minutes. Determine which group comes up with the larger number of different classifications.

WHEN: Before or after a lesson

CONTENT STANDARD(S):   Characteristics of organisms (K–4); Systems, order, and organization (K–12)

- Put two pieces of chart paper on the wall. Prior to the study of classification, have students brainstorm which animals are vertebrates and invertebrates. Then place five pieces of chart paper on the wall and ask students to name animals that are birds, amphibians, reptiles, mammals, or fish. For younger students, write the lists for them as they name the animals. Then following the study, have them make the lists again and compare the two.

WHEN: During a lesson

CONTENT STANDARD(S):   All (5–12)

- Teach students to know the difference between *minnow* or *skinny* questions and *whale* or *fat* questions. Skinny questions ask for quick recall of facts while whale questions call for students to analyze or explain facts or to predict based on previous knowledge. Have students use Bloom's Taxonomy Revised: Key Words, Model Questions, and Instruction Strategies (which appears at the end of this chapter) to formulate minnow and whale questions regarding a science topic for discussion. (Berman, 2008, pg. 10)

WHEN: During a lesson

CONTENT STANDARD(S):   All (5–12)

- Give students a science question to which there is more than one appropriate answer. Form cooperative groups of four to six students and brainstorm as many ideas as possible in a designated time period while complying with the following DOVE guidelines:
  - **D**efer judgment: Students should not comment positively or negatively on any of the brainstormed ideas. The goal is to get as many ideas as possible written down.
  - **O**ne idea at a time: Only one idea at a time is written down since students will be giving their full attention to the originator of each idea.
  - **V**ariety of ideas: Students should be encouraged to *think outside the box* and share original ideas.
  - **E**nergy on task: All students in each cooperative group should give their undivided attention to the task of brainstorming ideas and not to anything else at the time.

WHEN: During a lesson

CONTENT STANDARD(S):   Science as a human endeavor (5–12)

- Review the progress of inventions over the past 20 years. Put students in cooperative groups and have them discuss inventions that they are excited about. Have them brainstorm future inventions based on current technology and the benefits and consequences of each.

WHEN: During a lesson

CONTENT STANDARD(S):   All (K–12)

- Use the think, pair, share technique with students. Pose a question or discussion topic to the class. Have them *think* of an individual answer. Then have them *pair* with a peer and *share* their answer. Then call on both volunteers and nonvolunteers to respond to the entire class.

WHEN: During a lesson

CONTENT STANDARD(S):   Abilities necessary to do scientific inquiry (5–12); Evidence, models, and explanation (5–12)

- Before conducting an experiment in class, have students discuss the reasons for having a control group and an experimental group. Have them identify the variables and discuss which variable is being tested.

WHEN: During a lesson

CONTENT STANDARD(S):   Abilities of technological design (5–8); Systems, order, and organization (K–12)

- Bring in a variety of unique or antique kitchen gadgets. Put them in equal piles around the room. Have students form groups and rotate to visit each pile. Have them brainstorm and guess the function of each of the gadgets. Then, reveal the function for which the gadget was intended.

WHEN: During or after a lesson

CONTENT STANDARD(S):   All (K–12)

- When asking questions in class or creating teacher-made tests, provide opportunities for all students to be successful by asking both knowledge or short-answer questions and those that enable students to use their reasoning and critical- and creative-thinking skills. Refer to Bloom's Taxonomy Revised: Key Words, Model Questions, and Instruction Strategies (which appears at the end of this chapter) to ensure that students have opportunities to answer questions at all levels of the revised taxonomy, particularly those above the *knowledge* level.

WHEN: During or after a lesson

CONTENT STANDARD(S):   All (5–12)

- When reviewing for a test, have students brainstorm expected test questions. Then, have them review Bloom's Taxonomy Revised: Key Words, Model Questions, and Instruction Strategies (which appears at the end of this chapter) and categorize each question based on the appropriate level of questioning.

Bloom's Taxonomy Revised

Key Words, Model Questions, and Instructional Strategies

Bloom's Taxonomy (1956) has stood the test of time. Recently, Anderson and Krathwohl (2001) have proposed some minor changes to include the renaming and reordering of the taxonomy. This reference reflects those recommended changes.

I. REMEMBER (KNOWLEDGE)
(shallow processing: drawing out factual answers, testing recall, and recognition)

Verbs for Objectives	*Model Questions*	*Instructional Strategies*
Choose	Who?	Highlighting
Describe	Where?	Rehearsal
Define	Which one?	Memorizing
Identify	What?	Mnemonics
Label	How?	
List	What is the best one?	
Locate	Why?	
Match	How much?	
Memorize	When?	
Name	What does it mean?	
Omit		
Recite		
Recognize		
Select		
State		

(Continued)

Figure 1.1 (Continued)

II. UNDERSTAND (COMPREHENSION)
(translating, interpreting, and extrapolating)

Verbs for Objectives	Model Questions	Instructional Strategies
Classify	State in your own words.	Key examples
Defend	What does this mean?	Emphasize connections
Demonstrate	Give an example.	Elaborate concepts
Distinguish	Condense this paragraph.	Summarize
Explain	State in one word . . .	Paraphrase
Express	What part doesn't fit?	STUDENTS explain
Extend	What exceptions are there?	STUDENTS state the rule
Give Example	What are they saying?	"Why does this example . . . ?"
Illustrate	What seems to be . . . ?	Create visual representation (concept maps, outlines, flow charts organizers, analogies, pro/con grids) *PRO/CON*
Indicate	Which are facts?	
Interrelate	Is this the same as . . . ?	
Interpret	Read the graph (table).	Note: The faculty member can show them, but *they* have to do it.
Infer	Select the best definition.	Metaphors, rubrics, heuristics
Judge	What would happen if . . . ?	
Match	Explain what is happening.	
Paraphrase	Explain what is meant.	
Represent	What seems likely?	
Restate	This represents . . .	
Rewrite	Is it valid that . . . ?	
Select	Which statement supports . . . ?	
Show	What restrictions would you add?	
Summarize	Show in a graph, table.	
Tell		
Translate		

III. APPLY
(knowing when to apply; why to apply; and recognizing patterns of transfer to situations that are new, unfamiliar, or have a new slant for students)

Verbs for Objectives	*Model Questions*	*Instructional Strategies*
Apply	Predict what would happen if . . .	Modeling
Choose	Choose the best statements that apply.	Cognitive apprenticeships
Dramatize	Judge the effects.	"Mindful" practice—NOT just a "routine" practice
Explain	What would result?	
Generalize	Tell what would happen.	Part and whole sequencing
Judge	Tell how, when, where, why.	Authentic situations
Organize	Tell how much change there would be.	"Coached" practice
Paint	Identify the results of . . .	Case studies
Prepare		Simulations
Produce		Algorithms
Select		
Show		
Sketch		
Solve		
Use		

IV. ANALYZE (breaking down into parts, forms)

Verbs for Objectives	*Model Questions*	*Instructional Strategies*
Analyze	What is the function of . . . ?	Models of thinking
Categorize	What's fact? Opinion?	Challenging assumptions
Classify	What assumptions?	Retrospective analysis
Compare	What statement is relevant?	Reflection through journaling
Differentiate	What motive is there?	Debates
Distinguish	Related to, extraneous to, not applicable.	Discussions and other collaborating learning activities

(Continued)

Verbs for Objectives	Model Questions	Instructional Strategies
Identify	What conclusions?	Decision-making situations
Infer	What does the author believe?	
Point Out	What does the author assume?	
Select	Make a distinction.	
Subdivide	State the point of view of . . .	
Survey	What is the premise?	
	What ideas apply?	
	What ideas justify the conclusion?	
	What's the relationship between?	
	The least essential statements are . . .	
	What's the main idea? Theme?	
	What inconsistencies, fallacies?	
	What literacy form is used?	
	What persuasive technique?	
	Implicit in the statement is . . .	

V. EVALUATE (according to some set of criteria, and state why)

Verbs for Objectives	Model Questions	Instructional Strategies
Appraise	What fallacies, consistencies, inconsistencies appear?	Challenging assumptions
Judge	Which is more important, moral better, logical, valid, appropriate?	Journaling
Criticize		Debates
Defend	Find the errors.	Discussions and other collaborating learning activities
Compare		Decision-making situations

VI. CREATE (SYNTHESIS)
(combining elements into a pattern not clearly there before)

Verbs for Objectives	Model Questions	Instructional Strategies
Choose	How would you test . . . ?	Modeling
Combine	Propose an alternative.	Challenging assumptions
Compose	Solve the following.	Reflection through journaling

Verbs for *Objectives*	*Model Questions*	*Instructional Strategies*
Construct	How else would you . . . ?	Debates
Create	State a rule.	Discussions and other collaborating learning activities
Design		
Develop		Design
Do		Decision-making situations
Formulate		
Hypothesize		
Invent		
Make		
Make Up		
Originate		
Organize		
Plan		
Produce		
Role Play		
Tell		
Tell		

Figure 1.1   Key Words, Model Questions, and Instructional Strategies

Compiled by the IUPUI Center for Teaching and Learning. Revised December 2002. Used with permission from Purdue University, Indiana.

REFERENCES ■

Anderson, L. W., & Krathwohl, D. R. (2001). *A taxonomy for learning, teaching, and assessing.* New York: Addison Wesley Longman.

Bloom, B. S. (Ed.). (1956). *Taxonomy of educational objectives.* The classification of educational goals, by a committee of college and university examiners. New York: Longmans.

John Maynard, University of Texas, Austin

Marilla Svinicki, University of Texas, Austin

REFLECTION AND APPLICATION

How will I incorporate *brainstorming* and *discussion* into instruction to engage students' brains?

Which brainstorming and discussion activities am I already incorporating into my science curriculum?

What additional brainstorming and discussion activities will I incorporate?

Strategy 2

Drawing and Artwork

WHAT: DEFINING THE STRATEGY

Several years ago, I taught a science lesson where drawing was one of the major strategies used. It dealt with dominant and recessive genes. Since I had to get students' attention right away, I made the lesson relevant by telling these sixth graders the true story of my father's inherited trait for sickle-cell anemia, which he has passed to my older sister. My sister has passed it to her daughter. If my niece marries someone who also has the trait, they stand a very good chance of having an offspring with sickle-cell disease. I do not have the trait and neither does my daughter, Jennifer. However, Jennifer's daughter, my granddaughter Aidan, does have the trait. You should have seen students paying attention! One student even commented, "I'll really have to watch who I marry!" We then discussed how genes determine so much about us including the way we act, feel, and look. The culminating activity was to give students dominant and recessive traits of a set of parents and, based on their understanding of our discussion, have them draw what the offspring might look like. Students had so much fun comparing their drawings to one another's, and I had a blast teaching the lesson!

WHY: THEORETICAL FRAMEWORK

Even doodling and stick figures as drawings work very well as visual cues for memory and to change the state of students' brains during a lecture. (Jensen, R., 2008)

New content can be recalled better at a later time when students have the opportunity to add doodles or drawings while note taking. (Allen, 2008a)

All learners should be at least minimally exposed to a variety of ways to express their thoughts and feelings artistically and provided more formal instruction in some of those ways. (Jensen, R., 2008)

"If a picture is worth a thousand words, perhaps drawing and visualizing can help science students enhance their learning potential." (National Science Teachers Association [NSTA], 2006, p. 20)

Neurons can be wired for successful learning when children play—dance, draw, and sing—since every sense is engaged. (Sousa, 2006)

Paint the Picture is an activity that enables the teacher to give students a question and asks them to design a visual representation of their thinking that answers the question. It also points to the importance of scientists using representations to convey ideas. (Keeley, 2008)

Substituting art activities for other activities at any grade level and in any content area is fun and simple to do. (Sousa, 2006)

Drawing and other forms of artwork are great ways for students to express their emotions, channel their energy, manage their states, and subconsciously process content. (Jensen, R., 2008)

The success of the scientist and mathematician is taken from the skills of the artist such as spatial thinking, accurate observation, and kinesthetic perception. (Sousa, 2006)

The amygdala and the thalamus, two different areas of the brain, are both activated when people are engaged in art activities. (Jensen, E., 2001)

The brain is assisted in its search for meaning through the use of the patterns found in art, dance, music, and drama. (Fogarty, 2001)

Thinking in art precedes improvements in thinking in other curricular areas. (Dewey, 1934)

HOW: INSTRUCTIONAL ACTIVITIES

WHEN: Before or during a lesson

CONTENT STANDARD(S):   All (K–12)

- Have students build up academic vocabulary by creating a picture dictionary. Have them access their prior knowledge and make a prediction about what they think a new science vocabulary word means. Have them take a piece of notebook paper and fold it into four boxes labeled as follows: *My Prediction, Actual Meaning, Sentence,* and *Illustration.* Have students write the vocabulary word in the margin of the paper; and in Box 1, have them predict what the word means; in Box 2, have them write the actual meaning of the word; in Box 3, have them write a sentence using the word in context; and in Box 4, have them illustrate the meaning of the word. Have students place these sheets in a loose-leaf notebook so that new words can be added throughout the year.

WHEN: During a lesson

CONTENT STANDARD(S):   Characteristics of organisms (K–4), Reproduction and heredity (5–8)

- Have students draw an observation, such as the phases of mitosis (cell nuclear replication), seed germination, or beetle observation, in cartoon format with callout bubbles and talking captions.

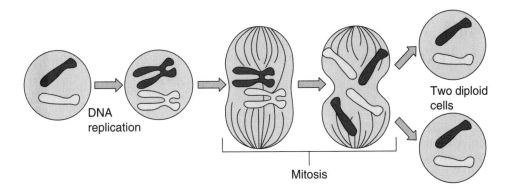

WHEN: During a lesson

CONTENT STANDARD(S):   Reproduction and heredity (5–8), Molecular basis of heredity (9–12)

- Using cutout shapes on colored paper for deoxyribonucleic acid (DNA) parts, have students construct a model of DNA using cytosine, guanine, adenine, and thymine shapes. After students have finished, have them connect all students' DNA together by twisting it into a chain. String the chain across the classroom and into the hall.

WHEN: During a lesson

CONTENT STANDARD(S):   Characteristics of organisms (K–4), Structure and function in living systems (5–8), Biological evolution (9–12), Form and function (K–12)

- Have students create leaf rubbings using real leaves. Have them place a piece of paper on top of the leaf and, with the side of their pencil, have them rub the paper to create an image of the leaf. They then label the lobes, blade shape, abscission layer, type of veining, and serrations. Have them write the name of the plant from which the leaf comes and the scientific name.

WHEN: During a lesson

CONTENT STANDARD(S):   Organisms and environments (K–4), Regulation and behavior (5–8), Behavior of organisms (9–12)

- Put students into cooperative groups. Give each group a live beetle and a worm, as well as a piece of paper. Have one person in each group draw and measure the paths of the beetle and worm as each crawls across the paper. Compare and graph the results as to the amount of time it took. Experiment with light and dark environments to see which one the beetles and worms prefer.

WHEN: During a lesson

CONTENT STANDARD(S):   Objects in the sky (K–4), Structure of the earth system (5–8), Origin and evolution of the universe (9–12)

- Have students use fluorescent paints to paint dots inside a film canister or a coffee can that would represent a constellation. Have them exchange their canister or can with a classmate's to learn many different constellations.

WHEN: During a lesson

CONTENT STANDARD(S):   Characteristics of organisms (K–4); Structure and function in living systems (5–8); Matter, energy, and organization in living systems (9–12)

- Divide students into cooperative groups. Give each group a different type of real flower. As students in each group dissect their flowers, have them draw and label the respective parts. Have them share their drawings with classmates from groups with different flowers.

WHEN: During a lesson

CONTENT STANDARD(S):   Characteristics of organisms (K–4); Structure and function in living systems (5–8); Matter, energy, and organization in living systems (9–12)

- Have students place leaves on sun-print, or light-sensitive, paper and put them in a sunny location. Have them label the leaf designs and identify the scientific names of the plants for a great classroom decoration.

WHEN:	During a lesson
CONTENT STANDARD(S):	Changes in earth and sky (K–4); Earth's history (5–8); Change, constancy, and measurement (K–12); Origin and evolution of the earth system (9–12)

- Have students make a flip book of a volcanic eruption. Have different students draw shield-volcano, composite-volcano, and cinder-cone-volcano eruptions to demonstrate a comparison.

WHEN:	During a lesson
CONTENT STANDARD(S):	Light, heat, electricity, and magnetism (K–4)

- To help them understand the concept of optics and particularly optical illusions, have students find and draw their own optical illusions or combine several different types in an original picture.

WHEN:	During a lesson
CONTENT STANDARD(S):	Organisms and environments (K–4), Diversity and adaptations of organisms (5–8), Biological evolution (9–12)

- Combine the strategies of manipulatives and discussion with drawing in the following activity. Have students mix cornstarch slowly with water until it forms a runny consistency, sometimes called *ooblech*. If students slap at the mixture, it will feel hard; but if they touch it slowly, their fingers will sink into it like quicksand. In small groups, have students brainstorm what adaptations an alien creature would have to make to live on a planet made of ooblech. Have them brainstorm the creature's features and then draw and describe the creature to the class.

WHEN:	During a lesson
CONTENT STANDARD(S):	Properties and changes of properties in matter (5–8); Structure and properties of matter (9–12); Systems, order, and organization (K–12)

- Have students make periodic-table squares on different pieces of cloth, and have them combine the squares into a quilt of the entire periodic table. Students can also make T-shirts of each element and arrange themselves into the periodic table.

WHEN: During a lesson

CONTENT STANDARD(S):   Properties of objects and materials (K–4), Properties and changes of properties in matter (5–8), Structure and properties of matter (9–12)

- Using a single sheet of paper, have students create a foldable booklet. An example of such a booklet can be seen at www.pocketmod.com. On the pages of the booklet, have students describe and draw the following: electron, proton, neutron, nucleus, atom, and molecule. This activity rank orders by size and will reinforce structure at the nanoscale.

WHEN: During a lesson

CONTENT STANDARD(S):   Structure and function in living systems (5–8), Molecular basis of heredity (9–12)

- Using a single sheet of paper, have students create a foldable booklet. An example of such a booklet can be seen at www.pocketmod.com. On the pages of the booklet, have students describe and draw the following: molecule, gene, DNA, chromosome, cell nucleus, and cell. This is a rank order by size and will reinforce structure at the micron scale.

WHEN: During a lesson

CONTENT STANDARD(S):   Evidence, models, and explanation (K–12)

- Have students use wood putty and work in cooperative groups to create a model of a cell, volcano, glacier, the earth's layers, and so forth on a piece of plywood. Each group creates a different model. Have them paint the models to make a resource that can be used year after year.

WHEN: During or after a lesson

CONTENT STANDARD(S):   Life cycles of organisms (K–4), Structure and function in living systems (5–8), Behavior of organisms (9–12)

- Have students place seeds on a wet paper towel and place the towel in a plastic sandwich bag. The seeds should be placed on the outside of the paper towel so that students can see the growth. Have students draw the growth of the seeds every day and label their parts as they grow.

REFLECTION AND APPLICATION

> How will I incorporate *drawing* and *artwork* into instruction to engage students' brains?

Which drawing and artwork activities am I already incorporating into my science curriculum?

What additional drawing and artwork activities will I incorporate?

Strategy 3

Field Trips

WHAT: DEFINING THE STRATEGY

One of the unique features of teaching in the DeKalb County School System in Decatur, Georgia, for more than 30 years was the numerous times I was able to experience one of the school system's greatest resources, the Fernbank Science Center. As a teacher, I escorted students to that wonderful place of learning. Fernbank afforded DeKalb students some of the richest scientific experiences available and was unique to the school system itself. Several times per year, students came on buses and spent the day touring the forest on the grounds and often attending labs with highly trained teachers of science. One of the most memorable features of the center, however, was the planetarium. Countless DeKalb students over the years took trips to the planetarium, leaned back in the comfortable chairs, and listened to informative narration while looking up in the night sky. Students learned about rotating and revolving planets, the North Star, the Big Dipper, the constellations, and a variety of other features of our real world. I would venture to say that students will not soon forget the experience of those field trips to Fernbank. The Fernbank Science Center was so successful, in fact, that years later the Fernbank Natural History Museum, including an IMAX theater, was built within the county and provided additional experiences for students in the area of natural history. The school system science fair was held at this museum where students could showcase their innovative projects, many of which went on to become state and national project winners.

Since brains were originally created to exist in the real world, it stands to reason that when students are acquiring information while experiencing a real-world environment, that information will be long remembered. Traditional school is very artificial to the brain. In fact, it is the only place I know where in some classrooms students are not allowed to engage in the very behaviors that come naturally to the brain while learning—to talk to one another and to move around in the environment. A field trip can ensure that both behaviors are addressed in an authentic and meaningful context.

WHY: THEORETICAL FRAMEWORK

An actual experience, such as a field trip, taps into a student's spatial memory, the place or time that something happened. (Fogarty, 2009)

As teachers start a new teaching unit, a field trip can be one useful tool since students need to see, touch, and experience the world and have real-world, concrete examples. (Gregory & Parry, 2006)

Reading about the zoo is not nearly as memorable as experiencing the smells, sounds, and images of the zoo. (Fogarty, 2009)

One way to integrate planned movement while learning content in the classroom is to take students on a field trip. (Sprenger, 2007)

Well-planned field trips are better than lab experiments in emulating good science since students formulate questions about nature, devise methods for answering the questions, implement the methods, evaluate the answers, and share the results with others. (Davis, 2002)

Critical-thinking skills can improve when students go into the real world and out of the classroom. (Jensen & Dabney, 2000)

Benefits of field trips include enhancing higher-order thinking skills, refining observation and questioning skills, and increasing the confidence of students. (Davis, 2002)

The class work of adolescents should carry them into the "dynamic life of their environments." (Brooks, 2002, p. 72)

Field trips, even virtual ones, create spatial memories, which are embedded in the brain and need no rehearsal. (Fogarty, 2001)

Not only association but also concrete experiences enable the brain to store a great deal of information. (Westwater & Wolfe, 2000)

Thousands of years ago, two of the world's greatest teachers, Aristotle and Socrates, used field trips as teaching tools. (Krepel & Duvall, 1981)

HOW: INSTRUCTIONAL ACTIVITIES

WHEN: Before a lesson

CONTENT STANDARD(S):   Objects in the sky (K–4), Earth in the solar system (5–8), Origin and evolution of the universe (9–12)

- Prior to a unit of study on the solar system, have students visit a planetarium where they actually see replicas of what they will be studying, including the stars, planets, and constellations.

WHEN: Before a lesson

CONTENT STANDARD(S):   Evidence, models, and explanation (K–12),
                                   Science as a human endeavor (K–12)

- Research a field-trip destination. Collaborate with colleagues and administration to come up with lists of museums, nature centers, and other activities related to science. Have students conduct virtual tours after their visit for other classes who visit.

WHEN: Before, during, or after a lesson

CONTENT STANDARD(S):   Evidence, models, and explanation (K–12); Understanding about scientific inquiry (K–12)

- Create an interdisciplinary unit around a field trip to a local beach, vernal pool, ecosystem, nature trail, botanical garden, and so forth. Integrate all of the disciplines into activities both prior to and after the field trip.

WHEN: During a lesson

CONTENT STANDARDS(S):   All (K–12)

- For a change of scenery, convene class outside on the school grounds. Allowing students to experience the positive effects of sunlight and the beauty of nature calms students' brains and puts the mind in a good state for learning. Conducting a class discussion while sitting under a tree can add a whole new dimension to instruction.

WHEN: During a lesson

CONTENT STANDARD(S):   Systems, order, and organization (K–12); Evidence, models, and explanation (K–12)

- Take students outside to draw on the sidewalk with chalk. Some possible ideas for the drawings could be food webs, food chains, glacial geology, systems of the human body, cell parts, and volcanic parts. If more than one class participates, students can go outside and observe what other classes have drawn. They can look for mistakes or additions to their chalk drawings.

WHEN: During a lesson

CONTENT STANDARD(S):   Evidence, models, and explanation (9–12), Understanding about scientific inquiry (9–12)

- Use an empty classroom to create a mock crime scene investigation (CSI) lesson. Using luminol, determine where blood was spattered and provide clues such as spilled supplies, toppled chairs, and so forth to allow students to brainstorm and re-create the "murder scene."

WHEN: During a lesson

CONTENT STANDARD(S):   Science as a human endeavor (5–12); Change, constancy, and measurement (5–12)

- Take the class outside. Use two poles connected by a two-meter string and a line level to determine the slope of a hill near your school. Have them find the differences in elevation, graph those differences, and make a slope formula from the results.

WHEN: During a lesson

CONTENT STANDARD(S):   All (K–12)

- Oftentimes, the classroom does not provide enough space for movement and games. Take the class outside and engage them in purposeful movement to reinforce a content objective or to play a game that requires more space than four walls will allow.

WHEN: During a lesson

CONTENT STANDARD(S):   Evidence, models, and explanation (K–12); Science as a human endeavor (K–12)

- Set up a scavenger hunt for students outside of the school building by having them locate answers to questions. At each question location, create a challenge activity for the group and provide a clue to help find the next location. This could be organized into a format similar to the *Survivor* TV show. Immunity idols can be hidden to add excitement to the game.

WHEN: During a lesson

CONTENT STANDARD(S):   Characteristics of organisms (K–4); Structure and function in living systems (5–8); The cell (9–12); Evidence, models, and explanation (K–12); Science as a human endeavor (K–12)

- Use your classroom as a field-trip destination. For example, decorate your classroom as a plant cell. Hang mobiles from the ceiling in the form of the cell nucleus, vacuoles, ribosomes, mitochondria, and so forth. Have students conduct tours for other classes who visit.

WHEN: During or after a lesson

CONTENT STANDARD(S):   Organisms and environments (K–4), Populations and ecosystems (5–8), Interdependence of organisms (9–12), Science as a human endeavor (K–12)

- Have students create a garden, butterfly garden, or a water garden at your school. Plant bulbs in the design of the school initials or logo. Label the more familiar names and the scientific names of the plants. Have students plan and conduct tours for other classrooms to visit the garden.

WHEN:	During or after a lesson
CONTENT STANDARD(S):	Changes in environments (K–4); Populations, resources, and environments (5–8); Environmental quality (9–12); Science as a human endeavor (K–12)

- Have students conduct a beach (or environmental) cleanup. Have them record the litter accumulated by type and amounts. Have them graph the results and notify the local newspaper for publicity.

WHEN:	During or after a lesson
CONTENT STANDARD(S):	Abilities necessary to do scientific inquiry (K–12), Understanding about scientific inquiry (K–12)

- Locate the nearest City Lab for a DNA investigation, Challenger Learning Center for a space simulation, or local college so that students can participate in a unique science-learning experience within the community.

WHEN:	During or after a lesson
CONTENT STANDARD(S):	Science and technology in local challenges (K–4); Science and technology in society (5–8); Science and technology in local, national, and global challenges (9–12); Understanding about science and technology (K–12)

- Set up a geocaching treasure hunt for students using a global positioning system (GPS). To find out more about geocaching, go to www.geocaching.com.

WHEN:	During or after a lesson
CONTENT STANDARD(S):	Evidence, models, and explanation (K–12); Science as a human endeavor (K–12)

- Invite local scientists and experts, including parents who have professions related to the science domains, to visit your classroom. Conduct an interview and videotape the interview. This could be shown on a local cable access channel (if permissions are obtained before airing the show).

WHEN:	After a lesson
CONTENT STANDARD(S):	Science and technology in local challenges (K–4), Science and technology in society (5–8), Environmental quality (9–12), Science as a human endeavor (K–12)

- Have students start a recycling program in your school. Locate outside agencies that will collect the classes' recycled materials in a dumpster outside of the school. There are often grants that can be secured that provide money to obtain recycling bins, wastebaskets, and rolling carts to help in the recycling process.

REFLECTION AND APPLICATION

How will I incorporate *field trips* into instruction to engage students' brains?

Which field trips am I already incorporating into my science curriculum?

What additional field trips will I incorporate?

Strategy 4

Games

WHAT: DEFINING THE STRATEGY

Students can't wait to get to science class today. The opening review activity is the game Password. If you remember the rules for the television show that was hosted by Allen Ludden, you will know how to play this game. The purpose of the game is to review the science vocabulary learned over the last few weeks. The class is divided into two heterogeneous teams. Each team sends two players to the front of the room who will face one another and play as partners. The object of the game is to be the first to get their partner to name a science word on the list by giving them a one-word clue. The clue cannot be a proper name, nor can any actions be used as the clue is given.

The word is *predator.* Team A begins. Partner 1 gives the clue *alien.* His partner answers *monster,* which is an incorrect response. If Team A had guessed the word, the team would receive 10 points; but since the word was not guessed, it moves over to Team B and is now worth 9 points. Partner 1 of Team B gives the clue *carnivore.* Her partner guesses *meat eater,* which is another incorrect response. The game shifts back to Team A for eight points, and the clue is *hawk.* The second member of Team B guesses *predator,* which is the correct response; so the team receives eight points, the value of the word at the time when it was guessed. If the word is not guessed by the time it is worth five points, the word is thrown out and a new word is used. Two new partners from each team are brought forward, and the game begins again with a new word from the list. Play continues until the time is up or until one team gets to a predetermined number of points.

Game playing is one of the ten things that keep people living beyond the age of 80, but games also create motivation and lessen the stress in your science classroom. They can be an excellent way to review concepts previously taught, but they also lower the *affective filter* of students. Engage your class in a spirited game of Jeopardy prior to a test, or toss a ball or Frisbee as students provide answers to review questions. Not only will retention of content increase, but students will actually look forward to coming to your science class every day!

WHY: THEORETICAL FRAMEWORK

When students have to memorize, practice, or rehearse important information, use games, puzzles, and other fun activities to make the content more creative. (Caine, Caine, McClintic, & Klimek, 2009)

Using game formats in class is motivating, lots of fun, and assists students in paying attention, focusing, and cooperating with one another. (Algozzine, Campbell, & Wang, 2009a)

The amount of time students are exposed to and involved with the content of a game is doubled when they develop the game's content along with playing it. (Allen, 2008a)

Certain games can be better than worksheets for reviewing content since they provide students with the necessary repetition and drill but are not boring. (Jensen, E., 2004)

Games enable students to work on social skills while helping them grow and develop cognitively. (Jensen, E., 2004)

Since games involve missing information, they stimulate students' attention. (Marzano, 2007)

Having students toss a ball while answering questions not only enables students to think and act quickly but also encourages problem solving, cooperation, and physical movement. (Jensen, E., 2004)

Endorphins, which stimulate the frontal lobes of the brain and give students a feeling of euphoria, are produced when students see their learning environment as positive. (Sousa, 2006)

Cortisol, a chemical that interferes with the recall of emotional memories, is produced when students see their learning environment as negative and stressful. (Kuhlmann, Kirschbaum, & Wolf, 2005)

For games to represent a form of review, they should focus on academic content. (Marzano, 2007)

When the teacher plans well, mild competition can facilitate student engagement; but when playing games, losing teams should not be faced with embarrassment. (Marzano, 2007)

Students enjoy writing questions for one another to be used when playing a game and require very little practice to do so. (Caine, Caine, McClintic, & Klimek, 2005)

If people are to be effectively motivated, the critical needs for survival, belonging and love, power, freedom, and fun must be satisfied. (Glasser, 1999)

HOW: INSTRUCTIONAL ACTIVITIES

WHEN: During a lesson

CONTENT STANDARD(S):   Characteristics of organisms (K–4); Structure and function in living systems (5–8); Matter, energy, and organization in living systems (9–12); Systems, order, and organization (K–12)

- Cut out and laminate pieces of the human body that, when assembled, combine to form a system of the human body. Also, cut out labels for the parts. Put students in cooperative groups, and give each group a set of parts and labels. Time how long it takes each group to arrange and correctly label each system. The winning group is the one who can assemble the system in the shortest amount of time. Have younger students assemble the body parts without the labels. When assembled, they can name each body part orally.

WHEN: During a lesson

CONTENT STANDARD(S):   Understanding about science and technology (K–12)

- This game is called Smack a Root. Tape squares to the wall in the front of the classroom. On each square is a science prefix, root word, or suffix. When students come across a prefix, root word, or suffix during the school year, have them run to the front of the room and, using a fly swatter, smack the word part. Points can be earned for each root smacked.

WHEN: During a lesson

CONTENT STANDARD(S):   All (K–12)

- Throw a soft football, Nerf ball, or stuffed animal around the room as science questions are randomly asked of students. Have students try to break the record of the most correct answers in a row.

WHEN: During a lesson

CONTENT STANDARD(S):   All (5–12)

- Conduct an Egg Carton Review. Write 12 review questions prior to a test, and place them in 12 numbered envelopes. Number the sections in an egg carton from 1 through 12. Place a marble in the egg carton and close it. Shake the carton. Have students take turns answering the questions on which the marble lands.

WHEN: During a lesson

CONTENT STANDARD(S):   All (K–12)

- Divide the class into two heterogeneous teams who compete against one another. Have students play Vocabulary Pictionary by taking turns coming to the front of the room, selecting a science word from a review pile, and drawing images on the board that would provide clues for their team to guess the word. The team to guess more words in an allotted time is the winner. For younger students, whisper in their ear the word that you want them to draw for the class.

WHEN: During a lesson

CONTENT STANDARD(S):   All (K–12)

- Create football, baseball, soccer, or basketball games using science questions to be reviewed prior to a test. Play the game according to the rules of the specific sport with more difficult questions worth more than easier ones.

WHEN: During a lesson

CONTENT STANDARD(S):   All (K–12)

- Have students play Autograph Bingo by having them collect autographs of classmates onto a blank bingo sheet. Place the name of each student on a small wooden craft stick, and put the sticks in a cup. Select a stick randomly from the cup and ask the student whose name has been selected a review question prior to a test. If the student answers the question correctly, the other students can claim that student's square on their individual bingo sheets. The first student to get bingo wins the game.

WHEN: During a lesson

CONTENT STANDARD(S):   All (5–12)

- Place students in groups of four to six. Give each group a set of cards with 15 science vocabulary words and their matching definitions. Have them mix up the words and definitions and place them facedown on a desk. Have students play the game of Concentration by matching science vocabulary definitions with their words.

WHEN: During a lesson

CONTENT STANDARD(S):   All (K–12)

- Have students work in groups to create an original game board out of oak tag. The game should review content prior to a test. Give each group a set of number generators (dice). Have student groups swap and play one another's completed games.

WHEN:	During a lesson
CONTENT STANDARD(S):	All (5–12)

- Have students participate in a People Search where they have to find answers to 12 short unfinished statements in a 4 × 3 grid drawn on a piece of paper. The statements should reflect content that you would like for students to review. For example, when studying the planets, you could use *Which one of the planets is the largest?* Students can supply only one answer for themselves. Then, they must get the remaining 11 answers from 11 different classmates. Play some fast-paced music and have students walk around the classroom getting answers from their peers. As peers provide answers, they initial each student's paper indicating that they provided the answer. At the end of the song, students should have 12 different initials, including their own, and the answers to all 12 statements. Review the statements with the entire class to be sure that all students have the correct answers.

WHEN:	During a lesson
CONTENT STANDARD(S):	All (K–12)

- Eggspert is an electronic game that determines which student hits the buzzer first. It is affordable and is an excellent addition to playing Jeopardy with the class. Jeopardy can be played using an all-play system where each student has a whiteboard, slate, or piece of paper. Students are put in heterogeneous groups or teams. When a question is asked, all students in the group must write down the answer to win. Students may tell others in their group the answer; but if they are too loud, other groups will hear. After all students have written the answer, the team captain can hit the buzzer on the Eggspert game.

WHEN:	During a lesson
CONTENT STANDARD(S):	All (5–12)

- Provide students with a bingo sheet containing 25 blank spaces. Have students write previously taught science vocabulary words or cell parts randomly in any space on their cards. Then, have students take turns randomly pulling from a bag and reading the definition of a designated word or part. Have students cover or mark out each word as the definition is read. The first student to cover five words in a row, horizontally, vertically, or diagonally, shouts out *bingo*. However, to win the student must orally give the definition for the five words that make up the bingo. If the student cannot supply the definitions, then play continues until a subsequent student wins.

WHEN: During a lesson

CONTENT STANDARD(S):   All (5–12)

- Using aluminum foil, roll strips into thin shapes that look and act like wires. Connect these wires to brass brads fastened to a piece of cardboard to create an electronic match board. Now, connect a light to a battery, so it lights up when the circuit is completed by touching the two ends on a correct match. Make label cards that fit onto a paper clip attached to the brads. Have students create matching questions and answers for any science unit that can be used on the light-up match board.

WHEN: During a lesson

CONTENT STANDARD(S):   All (K–12)

- Quizzillion Build Your Own Quiz Game is an electronic game that turns everyday quizzes into exciting interactive challenges for one to four players or teams. You can quickly and easily record multiple-choice or true-false questions into the main unit and then start up a quiz on any subject. Once the four wireless remote controls are handed out, Quizzillion asks all of the questions, reads out the answers (in your own voice!), and handles all of the scoring with engaging lights and sounds. You can choose either timed or untimed quiz challenges. Quizzillion even stores your quiz for play anytime you are ready. It offers three modes of play, including regular buzz-in play, random player selection, and live mode using buzz-in remotes without prerecorded quizzes, and keeps score automatically. (The game costs approximately $40 and is available through Learning Resources.)

WHEN: During a lesson

CONTENT STANDARD(S):   All (K–12)

- Purchase the CD *Classic TV Game Show Themes* so that you have the music that accompanies many of the games that you will play with your science class. The CD has the themes from the following game shows: *Wheel of Fortune, Jeopardy, Password, Family Feud, The Price Is Right,* and many more.

WHEN:	During a lesson
CONTENT STANDARD(S):	Understanding about science and technology (K–8)

- Go on the Internet; find and incorporate these Web-based game sites to enhance your science curriculum:
    o http://spaceplace.nasa.gov/en/kids/games.shtml
    o http://kids.nationalgeographic.com/Games
    o http://www.sheppardsoftware.com
    o http://pbskids.org/zoom/activities/sci
    o http://quizhub.com

WHEN:	During a lesson
CONTENT STANDARD(S):	All (K–8)

- Consult the series *Engage the Brain: Games* (a series of 10 books published by Corwin in 2008) for a plethora of additional game ideas across the curriculum. Books for Grades kindergarten through 5 are cross-curricular including games in the content areas of language arts, math, science, social studies, music, and physical education. There is a separate book for science in Grades 6 through 8.

REFLECTION AND APPLICATION

> How will I incorporate *games* into instruction to engage students' brains?

Which games am I already incorporating into my science curriculum?

What additional games will I incorporate?

Strategy   5

Strategy 5

Graphic Organizers, Semantic Maps, and Word Webs

WHAT: DEFINING THE STRATEGY

One of my favorite television shows is *Law and Order*. Obviously I am not alone since the series is one of the longest running of all time. It has been on the air for more than 20 years. Many times, I have watched police detectives take the information they have regarding a case and place it on a large board. Then, they draw lines to indicate what evidence is related to what suspects or which events happened in what sequential order or even in which locations. While examining the evidence as a whole, clues emerge that often lead to a conviction of the guilty party. One night while watching, it dawned on me that the pictures and drawings represent a graphic organizer. It is so much easier for the detectives to see how one piece of evidence relates to another when that evidence is depicted pictorially on the board. It is also so much easier for your students to see how science ideas are related when those ideas are shown through a concept, semantic, or mind map. Graphic organizers appeal to both left and right hemispheres of the brain and are, therefore, beneficial to all students. As you teach a science lesson, design a graphic organizer on the board, showing major concepts and details under each. Have students draw along with you, and watch their comprehension and retention improve. Those strong in left hemisphere can easily see the separate details of your lesson, and those strong in right hemisphere can view the major concepts simultaneously.

WHY: THEORETICAL FRAMEWORK

"Graphic organizers make thinking and learning visible." (Fogarty, 2009, p. 112)

According to the Institute for the Advancement of Research in Education (IARE), there are 29 research studies, all scientifically based, that champion the use of graphic organizers for improving student achievement across all grade levels, with diverse student populations, and in a variety of content areas. (IARE, 2003)

Graphic organizers help the learner create mental models, see relationships between concepts and apply those concepts, and link new learning to prior learning. (Hammerman, 2009)

Graphic organizers help a teacher structure interaction in a classroom that is brain-compatible. (Fogarty, 2009)

Mind maps, diagrams used to show relationships and organize information, are particularly helpful for students who are nonlinear thinkers. (Berman, 2008)

Types of graphic organizers include descriptive, sequential, process-causal, categorical, comparison-relational, problem-solution, and four-corner. (Hammerman, 2009)

A mind map, a type of graphic organizer, provides an exceptional way to evaluate students' thinking processes and reinforce their understanding of themes, relationships, and connections between ideas. (Jensen, E., 2008)

Graphic organizers can provide a teacher with a window into students' minds so that teaching can be customized to meet the specific needs of each student. (Jensen, E., 2004)

One of the most popular ways teachers can have students represent the knowledge that they have experienced is the graphic organizer, a form of *nonlinguistic representation*. (Marzano, 2007, p. 52)

When students occasionally create their own maps regarding new content, much frustration and confusion can be avoided. (Goldberg, 2004)

Mind maps enable students to arrange their thoughts into a format that they can easily understand. (Goldberg, 2004)

Mind maps enable children to consciously order their thinking and develop confidence for success with reading tasks. (Sylwester, 2003)

HOW: INSTRUCTIONAL ACTIVITIES

WHEN: Before, during, or after a lesson

CONTENT STANDARD(S):   All (K–12)

- To access students' prior knowledge before a science lesson is taught and summarize content after a lesson is taught, have students complete the K-N-L graphic organizer that follows. Have students discuss or brainstorm (1) what they already *know* about a concept or unit of study; (2) what they will *need* to know to comprehend the concept; and (3) following instruction, what they have *learned.* For younger students, have them dictate the answers as you write.

The K-N-L Strategy		
Topic:		
What I Know	What I Need to Know	What I Learned

WHEN: Before, during, or after a lesson

CONTENT STANDARD(S):   All (K–8)

- Refer to the series *Engage the Brain: Graphic Organizers and Other Visual Strategies* (a series of 9 books published by Corwin in 2008) to find additional graphic organizers in the content area of science. Grades K–5 have all content areas contained in the same book. Grades 6–8 have separate books for science. Consult the Corwin website at www.corwin.com.

WHEN: During a lesson

CONTENT STANDARD(S):   All (K–12)

- Since the brain thinks in chunks or connections, have students increase their knowledge of science vocabulary by using a word web. As new vocabulary is introduced, have students complete the word web that follows by brainstorming additional synonyms for the new word. Students can keep their word webs in a notebook for review and add synonyms throughout the year. Encourage them to add these words to their speaking and writing vocabularies as well.

Word Web

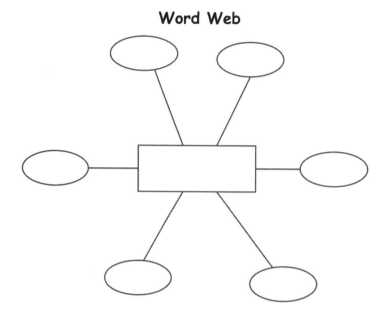

WHEN: During a lesson

CONTENT STANDARD(S):   Properties of objects and materials (K–4), Properties and changes of properties in matter (5–8), Chemical reactions (9–12), Abilities necessary to do scientific inquiry (K–12)

- Have students test various substances using a wide range of pH paper. Using a graphic organizer, called a pH scale, as a reference, have them place the recorded values on the scale.

WHEN: During a lesson

CONTENT STANDARD(S):   Changes in earth and sky (K–4), Earth's history (5–8), Origin and evolution of the earth system (9–12)

- Have students create a word web regarding continental and mountain glaciers. Have them write the types of features that each creates and connect them to the type of glacier.

WHEN: During a lesson

CONTENT STANDARD(S):   All (K–12)

- Have students use the cause-and-effect graphic organizer that follows to show causal relationships in science.

Cause/Effect

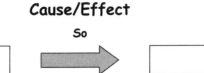

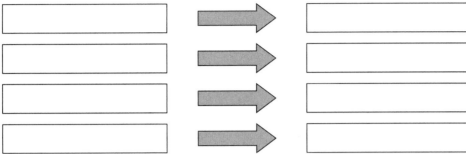

WHEN: During a lesson

CONTENT STANDARD(S):   Systems, order, and organization (K–12); Form and function (K–12)

- Have students collect various types of leaves and organize them onto a poster board that displays the various characteristics of each leaf. Have students connect the characteristics to create a dichotomous key.

WHEN: During a lesson

CONTENT STANDARD(S):   All (K–12)

- Have students complete the following sequence-of-events graphic organizer to show how one event leads to another in an experiment or in a real-life event.

Sequence

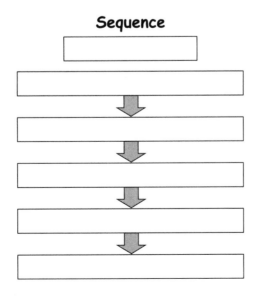

WHEN: During a lesson

CONTENT STANDARD(S):   Life cycles of organisms (K–4); Structure
                             and function in living systems (5–8);
                             Behavior of organisms (9–12); Evidence,
                             models, and explanation (K–12)

- Have students draw a graphic organizer depicting the life cycle of a monarch butterfly as it migrates from generation to generation. Graphic organizers can also show life cycles of plants, such as mosses or ferns.

WHEN: During a lesson

CONTENT STANDARD(S):   All (K–12)

- While lecturing or discussing scientific ideas with students, complete a semantic, concept, or mind map on the board to show how the major concepts are related to one another. Have students copy the map in their notes as you explain each part. See the sample format that follows:

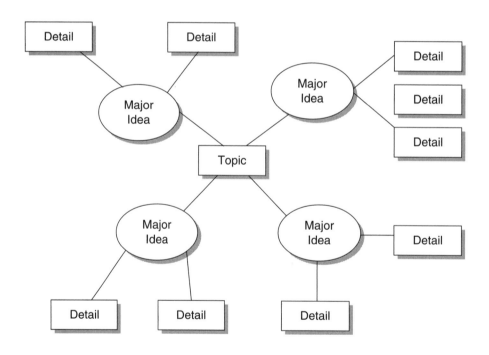

WHEN: During or after a lesson

CONTENT STANDARD(S):   Diversity and adaptations of organisms
                             (5–8), Molecular basis of heredity (9–12)

- Have students create a family tree of their own, noting similar and dissimilar traits in family members.

WHEN:	During or after a lesson
CONTENT STANDARD(S):	Abilities of technological design (5–12)

- Have students create a graphic organizer showing the manufacturing process of a product from raw materials to a finished packaged product. Products such as potato chips or paper clips could be researched.

WHEN:	During or after a lesson
CONTENT STANDARD(S):	Evidence, models, and explanation (K–12)

- Have students create a food web using various organisms in the ecosystem.

WHEN:	During or after a lesson
CONTENT STANDARD(S):	Abilities necessary to do scientific inquiry (5–12)

- Have students use a dichotomous key as a graphic organizer to identify specific plants and animals in the students' school area.

WHEN:	During or after a lesson
CONTENT STANDARD(S):	Earth's history (5–8), Geochemical cycles (9–12), Origin and evolution of the earth system (9–12)

- Have students create a concept map distinguishing the three types of volcanoes and the behaviors and resulting features of each type.

WHEN:	During or after a lesson
CONTENT STANDARD(S):	Reproduction and heredity (5–8), Molecular basis of heredity (9–12)

- Have students use a graphic organizer, called a Punnett square, to align hybrid and pure traits. Have them use the squares to predict outcomes of future generations for each trait.

WHEN:	During or after a lesson
CONTENT STANDARD(S):	Organisms and environments (K–4); Diversity and adaptations of organisms (5–8); Matter, energy, and organization in living systems (9–12)

- Have groups of students create a graphic organizer, called a food chain, for a particular animal such as a lion. Each group can use a different animal.

REFLECTION AND APPLICATION

> How will I incorporate *graphic organizers, semantic maps,* and *word webs* into instruction to engage students' brains?

Which graphic organizers, semantic maps, and word webs am I already incorporating into my science curriculum?

What additional activities will I incorporate?

Humor

WHAT: DEFINING THE STRATEGY

How do you tell the sex of a chromosome? (Just pull down its jeans/genes.)

An atom walks into a restaurant and says to the waiter, "I am so miserable, I have lost my electron." The waiter asks, "Are you sure?" The atom responds, "Yes, I'm positive!"

Why did the scientist have a knocker on his front door rather than a doorbell? (He wanted to receive the Nobel [no bell] Prize.)

What did the green grape say to the purple grape? (Breathe! Breathe!)

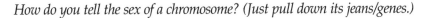

Did you like those riddles and that joke? If so, why not have more of them. After all, I got them from science teachers. If you teach older students, you probably have a class clown. The job of the class clown is to bring in appropriate riddles and jokes for the class. Periodically, either before, during, or after class, have a joke break. Laughter puts brains in a positive state and facilitates memory. Research (Allen, 2008a; Jensen, E., 2004) shows that jokes, riddles, celebrations, and other forms of positive interaction not only create a positive learning environment but may also facilitate the learning itself. Be sure not to confuse laughter with sarcasm. While a student might laugh following a sarcastic comment from a teacher or fellow student to save face, sarcasm actually tears down a student's confidence and higher-level thinking skills.

Laughter has an additional benefit. It has also been shown to produce T-cells, which strengthen the immune system and actually prolong life. The comedian Bernie Mac's early demise appears to be an exception and not the rule. As a rule, most comedians live beyond the age of 80. Consider the ages of the following comedians at the time of their deaths: George Burns, 103; Bob Hope, 100; Isabel Sanford, 86; Bea Arthur, 86; Soupy Sales, 83; and Rodney Dangerfield, 82. Consider also the ages of those who are still living above the age of 80: Phyllis Diller, Andy Griffith, Jerry Lewis, Cloris Leachman, and Betty White, just to name a few. Laughter in your classroom is just as good for you as for your students, both mentally and physically!

WHY: THEORETICAL FRAMEWORK

Activities that are fun should be used when appropriate since they provide mental breaks, enhance social relationships, and help to engage students. (Jensen, R., 2008)

The positive physiological effects of laughter include a decrease in pulse rate, an increase in oxygenation, and the production of endorphins (feel-good chemicals). (Costa, 2008)

Teachers who demonstrate a sense of fun and play and share jokes have students who feel positively about learning. This in turn can perpetuate a lifelong love of learning. (Jensen & Nickelsen, 2008)

The cognitive effects of laughter include a liberation of creativity and the fostering of the higher-level thinking skills of novelty, visualization, and making analogies. (Costa, 2008)

Learning should feel good, and all students should experience those feelings. (Zull, 2004)

Laughter lowers a student's stress level, strengthens the immune system, and increases the number of neurotransmitters that are essential if students are to remain alert and retain content. (Jensen, E., 2004)

When teachers loosen up, go with the flow, and have some fun in class, they will find that science is more playful and surprising than even the best toy! (Mangan, 2007)

"What we learn with pleasure, we never forget." (Allen, 2008a, p. 99)

Entertainment should be embraced by the teacher as a tool for delivering the objective and not the objective itself. (Jensen, R., 2008)

After the high of laughter, the body naturally relaxes into a state of calm; therefore, teachers can move students to a more quiet and focused state following a hearty laugh. (Allen, 2008a)

Even though some anxiety and low stress are necessary for most learning, a threatening classroom environment inhibits learning. (Caine & Caine, 2006)

When teachers periodically use humor, they show a sense of concern and cooperation. (Gettinger & Kohler, 2006)

Laughter provides students with a break in the class routine and can relax students who may be stressed. (Jensen, E., 2004)

The classroom must be an emotionally safe place for students if teachers want to lead them to the joyful end of the learning spectrum. (Faryadi, 2007)

Improvisational comedy enables students to think on their feet, puts a bit of fun and laughter into a lesson, and encourages students to take risks in front of their peers. (Udvari-Solner & Kluth, 2008)

When asked to identify the characteristics most preferred in a teacher, a sense of humor is included; a teacher who can communicate through a smile or a wink rather than a "premature expression of anger." (Sylwester, 2003)

HOW: INSTRUCTIONAL ACTIVITIES

WHEN: Before a lesson

CONTENT STANDARD(S):   All (K–12)

- Have teachers in a grade level or a department form a laughing club. There are over 1,800 such clubs in India alone, and since the brain does not know the difference between real laughter and fake laughter, they appear to work. The laughing club can meet before school long enough for a teacher to share a joke or riddle with the members. Teachers can take turns bringing the jokes for the week. Everyone gets their day off to a positive start, which can carry over into instruction.

WHEN: Before a lesson

CONTENT STANDARD(S):   All (5–12)

- Gather books of science jokes or others, such as elephant riddles, and have students pick the best jokes or riddles for a joke wall in the classroom. An example of an elephant riddle is as follows: *How can you tell that an elephant has been in your refrigerator? You can see his footprints in the butter!*

WHEN: Before a lesson

CONTENT STANDARD(S):   Form and function (5–12), Science as a human endeavor (5–12)

- Collect *Far Side* or similar comics that use animals and science. Create a wall in class or a collage of the cartoons and ask students to create their own similar ones. Students' cartoons can often be more creative than commercial ones.

WHEN: Before or during a lesson

CONTENT STANDARD(S):   All (K–12)

- Create science riddles by having students guess the answer. For example, describe an animal and have students answer the riddle *What animal am I?* Other riddles could include *What part of the human body am I? What ecosystem am I?* Then, have students write science riddles from content for one another to solve.

WHEN:	Before or during a lesson
CONTENT STANDARD(S):	All (5–8)

- Have students bring in jokes or riddles (preferably science jokes or riddles), have them write the jokes or riddles on index cards, and place them in a box. You might want to read them over prior to students placing them in the box to be sure they meet your approval. At the beginning of class or during a break in activity, draw a student's card from the box and let them tell their own joke or riddle.

WHEN:	Before, during, or after a lesson
CONTENT STANDARD(S):	All (5–12)

- Almost every middle and high school classroom has a *class clown.* Use that student to your advantage. Have them bring in science or other jokes or riddles to tell to the class. Make sure you approve of each joke before it is shared. Either before class, during the last few minutes, or at appropriate times during the period, have the class clown tell a joke. The entire class will laugh, putting each brain in a positive state for learning. The job of the class clown can rotate to other volunteers in the class each week until every student who wants a turn has had one.

WHEN:	During a lesson
CONTENT STANDARD(S):	All (K–12)

- Locate or create and incorporate cartoons, riddles, and jokes that reinforce concepts to be taught into the delivery of instruction. Here is one of Warren Phillips's favorite jokes. *There are so many ratings for various video games and movies that it can get confusing. I saw a rating for a very long movie the other day. It was rated PB4. Why? It was such a long movie that patrons were advised to PB4 (pee before you go in).*

WHEN:	During a lesson
CONTENT STANDARD(S):	Understanding about scientific inquiry (5–12)

- Try the following observation exercise. Say the following: *I am going to arrange the rulers and make a number. What's the number?* Arrange eight rulers carefully, and make a number with your fingers on the table. The students always look to the rulers to try to figure out the number when it is right in front of them (on your fingers)! This is a good lesson regarding how scientists sometimes miss the obvious when it is right in front of them. In addition, accidental discoveries often happen in this same way!

WHEN: During a lesson

CONTENT STANDARD(S):   All (K–12)

- Have students support and celebrate appropriate answers given by peers. These might include, but are not limited to, the following:
  1. Applause
  2. Thumbs-up
  3. High-fives
  4. Original cheers
  5. Standing ovations

Consult Chapter 17, "Celebrations," in the book *Shouting Won't Grow Dendrites: 20 Techniques for Managing a Brain-Compatible Classroom* (Tate, 2007) for more than 25 additional ways to celebrate student success in the classroom.

WHEN: During a lesson

CONTENT STANDARD(S):   All (K–12)

- Games help to reduce high stress in the classroom and can serve as wonderful ways to review science content prior to a test. Consult Strategy 4, Games, for additional ways to create laughter and fun in the science classroom.

WHEN: During or after a lesson

CONTENT STANDARD(S):   All (5–12)

- Have students design original cartoons, comic books, or superheroes to illustrate a key science concept previously taught. For example, students could design a comic book where the main character is *Proton Man,* a superhero with all the strengths and powers of a proton, or they could create a cartoon strip showing cell parts talking to one another.

WHEN: During or after a lesson

CONTENT STANDARD(S):   All (5–12)

- Use Warren Phillips's favorite science riddles for your students to solve. Use only those riddles that would be appropriate for the age and grade level of your students. Some of his suggested riddles are listed below:

What's the difference between a baked potato and pea soup? (Anyone can bake a potato.)

If there is H_2O inside a fire hydrant, what is on the outside? (K9P—canine pee)

What do you call a deer with no eyes? (No idea—no eye deer)

Where does a chemist put his dirty dishes? (Said with German accent) In the zinc!

Little Johnny's teacher asks, "What is the chemical formula for water?" Little Johnny replies, "HIJKLMNO!!" The teacher, puzzled, asks, "What on Earth are you talking about?" Little Johnny replies, "Yesterday, you said it was H to O!"

WHEN: During or after a lesson

CONTENT STANDARD(S):   All (K–12)

- Use the following websites as resources:
  www.basicjokes.com/dtitles.php?cid=16
  www.ahajokes.com/science_jokes.html
  www.xs4all.nl/~jcdverha/scijokes/index.html

REFLECTION AND APPLICATION

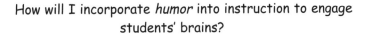

How will I incorporate *humor* into instruction to engage students' brains?

Which humorous activities am I already incorporating into my science curriculum?

What additional activities will I incorporate?

Strategy 7

Manipulatives, Experiments, Labs, and Models

WHAT: DEFINING THE STRATEGY

If you have ever taken one of my workshops, then you know that I am often asked about the last time I taught students in a classroom. I had the good fortune of observing a wonderful science lesson, which I later replicated with a group of students, and I often tell this story when I present. The lesson was as follows:

> To demonstrate the power of air pressure, each student was given a quart-size ziplock bag and a straw. They poked a small hole in the bag and stuck the straw through the hole. Then, they were told to put masking tape around the hole and zip up the bag so that the only air getting into the bag would come when they blew through the straw. Twelve students were then asked to come, bring their bags; and they and the bags were placed around a science table. Four students were put on both sides of the table and two on each end. The students crouched down so that they could blow through the straws. Then, the remainder of the class helped me turn another science table upside down so that the bags of the 12 students were between the two tables. Then, I stood on the top upside-down table with the goal being to have the 12 students blow into their bags simultaneously and attempt to raise me and the top table. When I taught this lesson, 12 sixth-grade students all blew at the same time and lifted me and the top table off of the bottom table. They were even able to do it with two adults standing on the top table. Try this experiment with your students. They will not only remember the demonstration, but they will have a new appreciation for the power of air pressure and this strategy.

Prior to conducting or having students conduct any of the following experiments, please heed this warning. Investigate the risks and hazards of each of the experiments before conducting it in class. It is your responsibility to provide a safe environment for all students. Practice each experiment prior to using it in front of a classroom full of students. Consult the Material Safety Data Sheets that accompany any chemicals used, and wear safety goggles and aprons when necessary.

WHY: THEORETICAL FRAMEWORK

Having students build models is a good way to assess their level of understanding of scientific principles and physical laws while simultaneously exploring, experimenting, and having fun. (Jensen, E., 2008)

Scientists in all fields use mental models (the solar system in astronomy, the DNA structure in biology, the atom in chemistry) to help students picture things that they are unable to directly observe. (Berman, 2008)

Since exercise and activity can enhance the growth of new cells in the brain, teachers should provide opportunities for students to "hold, mold, and manipulate clay or other objects." (Jensen, E., 2008, p. 38)

Manipulatives such as pipe cleaners, salt, Koosh balls, and toothpicks enable students to take advantage of their bodily-kinesthetic intelligence. (Karten, 2007)

The brain remembers best those visuals that are concrete and can be touched and manipulated. (Jensen, E., 2008)

Many students learn best with hands-on activities that enable them to manipulate physical objects and concepts. (Jensen, E., 2008)

Neural connections are more easily formed and information better remembered when learning is hands-on and active than when the students are watching the teacher do all the work and information is learned abstractly. (Gregory & Parry, 2006)

Students who use manipulatives over time increase their ability to discuss ideas, verbalize their thinking, take ownership, and find answers to problems independently. (Sebesta & Martin, 2004)

When students are involved in learning by inquiry, trial and error, and risk taking and where science activities are inspirational and hands-on, their brains operate at the highest level cognitively. (Fogarty, 1997)

There is not a single theory that adequately explains brain activity and the use of the hands since both are so complex and interconnected. (Jensen, E., 2001)

HOW: INSTRUCTIONAL ACTIVITIES

WHEN: Before or during a lesson

CONTENT STANDARD(S):   Abilities necessary to do scientific inquiry (K–12), Understanding about scientific inquiry (K–12)

- Create a science-toy table of manipulatives that students can play with as they first enter your classroom. This activity leads to many questions about how these gadgets work, and it keeps those very active students busy and eager to enter your room. Some favorite toys among Warren Phillips's students include magnetic drawing boards, metal puzzles, and motion toys such as gyro rings, gyroscopes, marble runs, Newton's cradle, and bottle connectors to create tornadoes. You can make your own science toys using ideas from the *Exploratorium Snackbook* (California Department of Education, n.d.). Many science catalogs also have science toys. One favorite catalog is *Educational Innovations*, from which many of the toys mentioned above are available for purchase (see www.teachersource.com).

WHEN: During a lesson

CONTENT STANDARD(S):   Reproduction and heredity (5–8), Molecular basis of heredity (9–12)

- Have students create a necklace with four colors of beads. The bead colors represent cytosine, guanine, adenine, and thymine, the four nitrogen bases in DNA. The pattern students make should represent a sequence of DNA. Students can then copy someone else's DNA, or even better, a best friend forever (BFF) could create a complementary strand. Matching every adenine with a thymine and every cytosine with a guanine does this. Students should compare base necklaces to ensure a perfect match.

WHEN: During a lesson

CONTENT STANDARD(S):   Properties of objects and materials (K–4), Properties and changes of properties in matter (5–8), Structure and properties of matter (9–12)

- Have students conduct the following experiment to demonstrate that there is space between molecules. Have students work in cooperative groups. Have each group measure out exactly 50 milliliters of water in a graduated cylinder. In another 100-milliliter graduated cylinder, have them measure out exactly 50 milliliters of ethyl alcohol. Have them pour the water into the ethyl alcohol cylinder. It should measure to about 83 milliliters, proving that some of the water fits between the larger alcohol molecules.

This same effect can be demonstrated by adding 50 milliliters of fine sand to 50 milliliters of marbles in a 250-milliliter graduated cylinder. The fine sand will fit between the marbles so that the total does not add up to 100 milliliters. You can also add 50 milliliters of water and see that the water fills in other spaces, so the total is not 150 milliliters.

WHEN:	During a lesson
CONTENT STANDARD(S):	Matter, energy, and organization in living systems (9–12); Understanding about scientific inquiry (K–12); Evidence, models, and explanation (K–12)

- Using tongs, burn a Pringles potato chip. (Be sure to have goggles, matches, a lab apron, and fire extinguisher handy.) Have students observe the tremendous amount of energy it contains as it burns for almost two minutes. Have them also observe the liquid fat come out of the chip as it burns, similar to candle wax burning. Rotating the chip as it burns allows it to burn longer. This also demonstrates calories, as energy amounts in the food we eat. From that point on, students will want to look at *fat calories* in different products. Peanuts also burn well as do other potato chips. Students could compare the amount of time each product burns. However, they must take surface area into consideration.

WHEN:	During a lesson
CONTENT STANDARD(S):	Motions and forces (5–8); Transfer of energy (5–8); Interactions of energy and matter (9–12); Understanding about scientific inquiry (K–12); Evidence, models, and explanation (K–12)

- Stretch out a metal Slinky across the room. At the far end of the room, attach a round can (a Pringles potato chip can works well) to the Slinky. Rap the Slinky with a metal pen and have students hear the amplified sound at the opposite end of the room. A string wrapped around the Slinky and pressed against the ears of students will create a stereo sound when the Slinky is tapped.

  Then, do a demonstration by pulling a section of the stretched Slinky and releasing it quickly. The resulting wave can be seen traveling across the room and returning to where it was made. This demonstrates a compression wave, which is how sound actually travels. The return wave demonstrates the concept of an echo. Be very careful of students' fingers and wear goggles when releasing the Slinky in any experiment as injury can occur if it is released on an unsuspecting observer.

WHEN: During a lesson

CONTENT STANDARD(S):   Position and motion of objects (K–4); Motions and forces (5–8); Transfer of energy (5–8); Interactions of energy and matter (9–12); Conservation of energy and increase in disorder (9–12); Understanding about scientific inquiry (K–12); Evidence, models, and explanation (K–12)

- Put a small dish of water on an overhead projector or a document camera. Strike a tuning fork to make it vibrate. Put the tuning fork in the water. All students will be able to see the vibrations as they travel through the water.

WHEN: During a lesson

CONTENT STANDARD(S):   Characteristics of organisms (K–4); Structure and function in living systems (5–8); Behavior of organisms (9–12); Understanding about scientific inquiry (K–12); Evidence, models, and explanation (K–12); Personal health (K–8)

- To demonstrate the concept of peristalsis, the action of the muscles in the throat, have a student volunteer to do a headstand and drink water through a straw while the class observes. Students will notice that the throat muscles squeeze the water into the stomach very much like pressing the sides of a toothpaste tube. They will learn that gravity is not necessary for swallowing.

WHEN: During a lesson

CONTENT STANDARD(S):   Structure of the earth system (5–8); Origin and evolution of the earth system (9–12); Understanding about scientific inquiry (K–12); Evidence, models, and explanation (K–12); Evolution and equilibrium (K–12)

- For this experiment, you will need an entire roll of Mentos and a two-liter bottle of diet cola. Unwrap the whole roll of Mentos and position them directly over the mouth of the bottle of diet cola so that all of the candies can drop into the bottle at the same time. CO_2 will be released, sending the soda about 10 feet in the air. Have students come up and try varying numbers of Mentos, measuring eruption heights and times. This is best done as an outdoor experiment. Be sure that students have goggles and a lab apron.

WHEN:	During a lesson
CONTENT STANDARD(S):	Properties of objects and materials (K–4), Properties and changes of properties in matter (5–8), Chemical reactions (9–12)

- Create an oxidation laboratory by showing students that oxygen is actually very reactive and that steel can burn. Obtain four different types of steel wool (0, 00, 000, 0000) from your local hardware store, and conduct this experiment in the science lab or outdoors. Tear off a small section of each of the steel wools. Hold the steel wool with tongs. With a match, light the various types of steel wool. (Be sure to have goggles, a lab apron, and fire extinguisher handy in a ventilated area.) The finer steel wools will burn much better than the thicker ones because they have more surface area to react with oxygen. Blowing on the steel wool will add more oxygen. Help students to realize that we also breathe out some oxygen as well. This experiment will show students a chemical change.

$$(2Fe + O_2 \rightarrow 2FeO)$$

WHEN:	During a lesson
CONTENT STANDARD(S):	Motions and forces (5–12); Understanding about scientific inquiry (K–12); Evidence, models, and explanation (K–12)

- You must do this great air-pressure demonstration with the class! Bring in a hard-boiled egg. Peel off the shell. Place about 10 matchsticks into the top of the egg. Find a milk bottle. (Be sure to have your goggles, lab apron, and fire extinguisher ready.) Light one of the match sticks and quickly place the egg up snug against the *inverted* milk bottle. The egg will be pushed up into the bottle, defying gravity! Warren calls this the birthday egg, and the class sings "Happy Birthday" as the egg gets pushed into the bottle. This lab demonstrates that hot air has fewer molecules, and is less dense, than colder air. As the air in the bottle heats up, it has fewer atoms of oxygen. The atoms outside the bottle push their way into the bottle by forcing the egg into the bottle. Tell students that average air pressure is about 14.7 pounds per square inch at sea level. That's a lot of force! Can you get the egg *out* of the bottle once it's in there? Sure! Just invert the bottle so that the egg is pressing against the opening. Now, blow quickly and hard into the bottle. The resulting air pressure you create in the bottle will push the egg back out!

| **WHEN:** | During a lesson |
| **CONTENT STANDARD(S):** | Properties of objects and materials (K–4); Properties and changes of properties in matter (5–8); Chemical reactions (9–12); Understanding about scientific inquiry (K–12); Evidence, models, and explanation (K–12) |

- Place a candle in a small, clear plastic container and light it. (Be sure to have your goggles, lab apron, and fire extinguisher handy.) Put a beaker of vinegar in the container. Add baking soda and have the class watch gas escape. The gas is carbon dioxide (CO_2), and it will sink to the bottom of the container. When enough of the CO_2 gas accumulates in the container, the flame will be extinguished.

| **WHEN:** | During a lesson |
| **CONTENT STANDARD(S):** | Organisms and environments (K–4); Populations and ecosystems (5–8); Behavior of organisms (9–12); Understanding about scientific inquiry (K–12); Evidence, models, and explanation (K–12) |

- Sodium polyacrylate, better known as *ghost crystals,* is a super-absorbing polymer available from science supply sources, such as Educational Innovations (see www.teachersource.com). When placed in distilled water, these crystals are invisible since they have the same index of refraction as the water. Have students place these crystals into clear glasses and grow plants in them. Students can then see all the parts of the plants without the soil. (Sodium polyacrylate is also used and available in baby diapers and at garden centers where the crystals serve as water reservoirs.)

  Play the shell game with students by getting three styrofoam cups and adding sodium polyacrylate to just one of the cups. Add water to the same cup. Move the cups around. The polymer will absorb the water, so none of the containers appear to have any water in them. Won't your students be surprised?

| **WHEN:** | During a lesson |
| **CONTENT STANDARD(S):** | Properties and changes of properties in matter (5–8); Structure and properties of matter (9–12); Understanding about scientific inquiry (K–12); Evidence, models, and explanation (K–12) |

- Show students that when you spray compressed air from a can, like the ones used to clean computer parts, it changes from a liquid to a gas. Since liquids have less energy than gas, as the gas is created, the can cools off dramatically. The air takes energy from its surroundings, causing the can to feel cold. Remind students that they should *never* inhale the air from cans like these. This demonstration can accompany the song "The States of Matter" found in Strategy 11: Music, Rhythm, Rhyme, and Rap.

WHEN:	During a lesson
CONTENT STANDARD(S):	Light, heat, electricity, and magnetism (K–4); Transfer of energy (5–8); Interactions of energy and matter (9–12); Understanding about scientific inquiry (K–12); Evidence, models, and explanations (K–12)

- Lasers make a great demonstration of the law of optics but are for teacher use only! Take a two-liter bottle and make a small (about ½ inch) hole in it about four inches from the bottom. Put adhesive tape over the hole, and fill the bottle with water and a tiny bit of milk mixed together. Shine the laser through the bottle and aim it at the hole on the other side. Release the tape. The laser will follow the leaking water as it curves out of the bottle. Emphasize that light always travels in a straight line, but here it is bouncing back and forth within the stream of water. You can show students total internal reflection as the laser bounces off the top and bottom of a rectangular acrylic shape. You can also arrange mirrors to hit a target, showing students the law of reflection, or emphasize the use of fiber optics in communication by shining a laser into a fiber-optic cable and having students note the light at the other end of the cable.

WHEN:	During a lesson
CONTENT STANDARD(S):	Science and technology in local challenges (K–4); Risks and benefits (5–8); Environmental quality (9–12); Understanding about scientific inquiry (K–12); Evidence, models, and explanation (K–12)

- Starch packing peanuts are biodegradable and will dissolve in water. Varying the water temperature makes for an interesting experiment from which you can have students predict the results. Students can graph the results (the *time* it takes for peanuts to dissolve versus the *temperature* of water) and make a slope to predict future experiments.

WHEN: During a lesson

CONTENT STANDARD(S):   Light, heat, electricity, and magnetism (K–4); Transfer of energy (5–8); Motions and forces (5–12); Interactions of energy and matter (9–12); Evidence, models, and explanation (K–12); Understanding about scientific inquiry (K–12)

- Get an Energy Ball, which is available from Educational Innovations (see www.teachersource.com). This interesting device consists of a 1.5-inch ball with two small metal electrodes. When the two electrodes are touched simultaneously, the device flashes and makes a pleasing warbling sound. The Energy Ball utilizes a field transistor, so even the slightest conduction between the two electrodes activates the sphere. The Energy Ball is completely self-contained and requires no additional batteries or energy source. Use it to demonstrate closed and open circuits by having two students each touch a different electrode and then activate the device by holding hands. It also shows that humans conduct electricity and that electromagnetic energy flows through our bodies. This electromagnetic current can even travel through all of the students in your class!

WHEN: During a lesson

CONTENT STANDARD(S):   Transfer of energy (5–8); Interactions of energy and matter (9–12); Understanding about scientific inquiry (5–12); Evidence, models, and explanation (5–12); Understanding about science and technology (5–12)

- Demonstrate total reflection to the class by bouncing a laser off the top of a rectangular acrylic shape or by creating a maze with a target at the end. Using the laser, arrange mirrors in the latter demonstration to hit the target. You can even shine a laser into a fiber-optic cable. Have students note the light at the other end of the cable. Emphasize the use and importance of fiber optics in communication.

REFLECTION AND APPLICATION

> How will I incorporate *manipulatives, experiments, labs,* and *models* into instruction to engage students' brains?

Which manipulatives, experiments, labs, and models am I already incorporating into my science curriculum?

What additional activities will I incorporate?

Metaphors, Analogies, and Similes

WHAT: DEFINING THE STRATEGY

A science teacher was teaching the steps in the scientific process. Her lesson could have been *as dull as dirt.* However, she had a burst of insight that made it one of the better lessons she had taught. Instead of just explaining the steps to teenagers, she compared them to the phases of a relationship with a new boyfriend or girlfriend. For example, when you first meet that person, you form a hypothesis or prediction about them, then you have to gather relevant data to prove or disprove your original hypothesis, and finally you reach a conclusion as to whether this person is one you will want to date. During the relationship, you are constantly gathering data that assist in accepting or rejecting the original hypothesis. By making the steps in the scientific process analogous to starting a new relationship, it immediately became relevant and made sense to high school students.

Metaphors, analogies, and similes are everywhere in the real world. Even in the first paragraph of this chapter, I inadvertently used a simile, *dull as dirt*, to compare a boring science lesson to the uninteresting characteristics of soil. Since the brain retains information by forming connections, this strategy is invariably powerful for understanding and long-term memory. Try the following experiment on family members. Hold up a piece of white paper and ask them the following question: *What color is this paper?* They should respond orally, *White.* Then quickly ask them, *What do cows drink?* The answer you will probably get is *Milk* when your family members know full well that cows drink water. What do you think happened? That's right! Their brains connected the word *white,* which was sitting in short-term memory from the first question, to the words in the second question, *cow* and *drink.* The connection, of course, was *milk.* Teach unknown science concepts metaphorically by connecting them to known ones and watch the effectiveness of this teaching tool!

WHY: THEORETICAL FRAMEWORK

A variety of concepts from the field of physics (such as force, momentum, inertia, and orbit) are used as metaphors and analogies to help students understand other subjects. (Caine, Caine, McClintic, & Klimek, 2009)

Content becomes more coherent when students use metaphor and analogy, two semantic transformations, to explain a concept. (Jensen, E., 2009, p. 56)

Synectics, having students use analogies or metaphors to connect ideas to a concept, can be used to engage students in creatively linking new information to prior knowledge. (Keeley, 2008)

Teachers can introduce new knowledge using metaphors and analogies since the frame of reference can be shifted when one concept is used to explain something else. (Caine, Caine, McClintic, & Klimek, 2009)

Acronyms can be rather effective for recalling lists but can be more useful for certain content and for certain learners. (Jensen, R., 2008)

Analogies are invaluable since they can give insight into students' misconceptions and inaccuracies regarding their content knowledge. (Keeley, 2008)

Analogies allow students to use multiple parts of their brains to form connections or links and are very effective for making abstract concepts memorable and more tangible. (Jensen, R., 2008)

Metaphor takes something tangible to describe something conceptual and uses the familiar to explain something unfamiliar. (Jones, 2008)

Two of the four types of tasks students should use to identify similarities and help them develop knowledge are creating metaphors and creating analogies. (Marzano, 2007, p. 64)

Students make pertinent connections and increase their comprehension of content when analogies are used to clarify or explain ideas. (Gregory & Parry, 2006)

The majority of concepts are understood only in relation to other concepts. (Lakoff & Johnson, 1980)

HOW: INSTRUCTIONAL ACTIVITIES

WHEN:	Before a lesson
CONTENT STANDARD(S):	All (K–12)

- Have students make predictions before a unit of instruction begins using the simile format. Put the following on the board: *How do you think the topic _____ is like a _____?* Fill in the simile for the students. For example, *How do you think the layers of the earth are like a hard-boiled egg?* Have students then use their background knowledge to make a connection. Have them revisit the predictions at the end of the lesson.

WHEN:	During a lesson
CONTENT STANDARD(S):	Characteristics of organisms (K–4); Structure and function in living systems (5–8); The cell (9–12); Evidence, models, and explanation (K–12)

- Compare an animal cell to a kingdom. All the parts of an animal cell are alive, so they compare to living members of the kingdom. For example, the king would be the nucleus and the power plant workers are the mitochondria. In a plant cell, the cell wall is not alive, much like the stone wall around the kingdom. Label or have students label all the parts of the cell and compare them to a member of the kingdom.

WHEN:	During a lesson
CONTENT STANDARD(S):	Changes in earth and sky (K–4), Earth in the solar system (5–8), Origin and evolution of the earth system (9–12)

- When teaching the layers of the earth's sediment, have students compare those layers to the dirty clothing deposited in a laundry basket. The most recent deposits would be on the top in both instances.

WHEN:	During a lesson
CONTENT STANDARD(S):	Abilities necessary to do scientific inquiry (K–12); Change, constancy, and measurement (K–12); Understanding about science and technology (K–12)

- Compare a local ecosystem to another exotic or extreme one in another part of the world. This can be accomplished by using online learning communities, such as e-Pals Global Community (2010, www.epals.com) or the National Geographic (n.d.) Jason Project (www.jason.org/public/whatis/start.aspx), where students work side by side with other students and scientists. (The e-Pals website provides an online network for schools to engage in collaborative, project-based learning. Learners can connect locally, nationally, or internationally. The Jason Project connects students with scientists and science events. Students can connect their knowledge to real-world scenarios faced by scientists.)

WHEN: During a lesson

CONTENT STANDARD(S): Structure and function in living systems (5–8); Reproduction and heredity (5–8); Molecular basis of heredity (9–12); Understanding about scientific inquiry (5–12); Evidence, models, and explanation (5–12)

- To help students understand the sheer enormity of DNA tell them if you took all the DNA strands in one human cell and stretched it out, it would extend a few meters. But there are approximately 10 trillion cells in the human body. Therefore, the entire DNA in the human body, if laid end to end, would reach from the earth to the sun a hundred times!

WHEN: During a lesson

CONTENT STANDARD(S): Properties of objects and materials (K–4); Properties and changes of properties in matter (5–8); Structure and properties of matter (9–12); Understanding about scientific inquiry (K–12); Evidence, models, and explanations (K–12)

- Use the following simile to help students understand the vast number of molecules in water: A thimble full of water contains as many molecules as the Atlantic Ocean contains thimblefuls of water.

WHEN: During a lesson

CONTENT STANDARD(S): Changes in earth and sky (K–4), Earth in the solar system (5–8), Origin and evolution of the earth system (9–12), Evolution and equilibrium (K–12)

- Compare the earth to an apple. Tilt the apple to represent a 23.5-degree angle of tilt of the earth. Rotate the apple on its axis and revolve it around an imaginary sun to simulate a day and a year. Cut the apple to show the core, mantle, and crust. Every time your students eat an apple, they will be reminded of the earth.

WHEN: During a lesson

CONTENT STANDARD(S):   All (5–12)

- To encourage creative thinking, have students complete a cloze sentence such as the following: *If _____ were a _____, it would be _____ because _____.* For example, if *the brain* were *a piece of jewelry,* it would be a *chain* because *it has many links.*

WHEN: During a lesson

CONTENT STANDARD(S):   Position and motion of objects (K–4); Motions and forces (5–8); Structure and properties of matter (9–12); Evidence, models, and explanation (K–12)

- To help students appreciate the infinite number of atoms in the universe, tell them that there are more atoms on a speck of dust than there are people on earth, approximately seven billion.

WHEN: During a lesson

CONTENT STANDARD(S):   Properties of objects and materials (K–4), Transfer of energy (5–8), Interactions of energy and matter (9–12), Form and function (K–12)

- Tell students that resonating sounds are very much like *a kid on a swing.* If sounds occur at just the right time and place, they increase the push dramatically. For example, an atom vibrates at a certain frequency. If many of the same kinds of atoms are located in a *pure* substance, they will resonate together at a certain frequency. The substance can even vibrate so much that it will shatter.

WHEN: During a lesson

CONTENT STANDARD(S):   Matter, energy, and organization in living systems (9–12); The cell (9–12); Understanding about scientific inquiry (K–12); Evidence, models, and explanation (K–12)

- Remind students that when they separate an egg's white from its yolk and pour the egg white on a hot griddle, it changes from a liquid to a solid, while most substances change from a solid to a liquid when heated. Tell them that the protein, or albumin, in the egg unravels to form a solid. Compare this to what happens when you get a cut and begin bleeding. The protein in the blood, or fibrinogen, unravels to form a scab by attaching itself to white blood cells. Point out to students that when they take the egg yolk and put it on the griddle, it doesn't change since it has a membrane that keeps its contents together, much like a cell membrane does.

WHEN:	During a lesson
CONTENT STANDARD(S):	Properties and changes of properties in matter (5–8), Structure of atoms (9–12)

- Bohr's model of the atom can be likened to a hotel with no elevators. Tell students that the electrons will fill the first floor before they have to move to the next floor. The first floor holds only two electrons, the second floor holds eight, the third floor holds eight, and so forth.

WHEN:	During a lesson
CONTENT STANDARD(S):	Characteristics of organisms (K–4); Structure and function in living systems (5–8); Matter, energy, and organization in living systems (9–12); Understanding about scientific inquiry (K–12); Evidence, models, and explanation (K–12)

- Students need to know that the heart pumps blood only through large blood vessels. Help them understand that if it pumped *all* over the body, when they got a cut, blood would shoot out across the room like a garden hose being squeezed. It is capillary action that does most of the work in bringing blood to cells. Let them know that we have two billion capillaries in our bodies, enough to supply oxygen and food to every cell.

WHEN:	During a lesson
CONTENT STANDARD(S):	Changes in earth and sky (K–4), Earth's history (5–8), Structure of the earth system (5–8), Energy in the earth system (9–12), Geochemical cycles (9–12), Origin and evolution of the earth system (9–12), Origin and evolution of the universe (9–12)

- The earth's continents float on the liquid mantle creating plate tectonics. To help students visualize this, liken the earth to a pot of simmering tomato soup with large crackers floating on it. The crackers will move slowly and occasionally bang into each other, sometimes submerging, much like the continents. If you simmer tomato soup with crackers on a hot plate for the class, this demonstration can also serve as a visual.

WHEN: During a lesson

CONTENT STANDARD(S):   Types of resources (K–4); Changes in environments (K–4); Risks and benefits (5–8); Natural hazards (5–8); Populations, resources, and environments (5–8); Environmental quality (9–12); Population growth (9–12); Natural and human-induced hazards (9–12)

- Have students compare the earth to an apple. Provide the following demonstration. Cut the apple into four quarters. Three of those quarters represent the ocean. Name the oceans, eat the three parts, and discard the apple. The fourth quarter represents the continents. Name the continents. Now cut the fourth quarter in half (one-eighth of the apple). This represents inhospitable land. Eat and discard. Now, cut the remaining piece in half (one-sixteenth of the apple). This represents land that is too wet, steep, or arid to inhabit for most people. Eat and discard. Now, cut the remaining piece in half (one thirty-second of the earth). This represents land that is not used for one reason or another (too remote, National Parks, or open land). Eat and discard. Now with the one thirty-second piece left, peel off the skin. This represents the productive surface that supports more than six billion people. It looks, and is, very fragile. It is also the most polluted segment of all of the pieces shown. This is an excellent metaphor for how limited the resources on earth are and how we must protect our planet. Warren uses this excellent activity as an opening lesson for his science classes every year! He also makes a point to have an apple on his desk each day thereafter as a reminder!

WHEN: During or after a lesson

CONTENT STANDARD(S):   All (5–12)

- To assist students in comprehending the relationship between two concepts in science, have them create analogies. Give them the pattern A : B :: C : D (A is to B as C is to D) to show how two sets of ideas or concepts are related. For example, Eli Whitney : the cotton gin :: Thomas Edison : the lightbulb. Once they get the hang of it, students can then create their own analogies, leaving a blank line for other students to complete.

REFLECTION AND APPLICATION

How will I incorporate *metaphors, analogies,* and *similes* into instruction to engage students' brains?

Which metaphor, analogy, and simile activities am I already incorporating into my science curriculum?

What additional activities will I incorporate?

Strategy 9

Mnemonic Devices

WHAT: DEFINING THE STRATEGY

Mnemonic devices are acronyms and acrostics, and while they may not necessarily equate with higher-level thinking, they can be used as effective tools for remembering. As a matter of fact, the word *mnemonic* comes from the Greek word *mnema*, which means memory. Let's consider the following scientific acrostics: To remember the planets in order from the sun, one only had to recall, *My Very Educated Mother Just Served Us Nine Pizzas*, which stood for Mercury, Venus, Earth, Mars, Jupiter, Saturn, Uranus, Neptune, and Pluto. Since 2006, when *planet* was redefined in such a way as to exclude Pluto, I have changed the acrostic to *My Very Educated Mother Just Served Us Nachos*. To recall the colors of the visible light spectrum from least energy to most energy, the acronym ROY G. BIV suffices (red, orange, yellow, green, blue, indigo, and violet). There has been some discussion that perhaps indigo and violet should be combined as one color, but most references still list seven colors of the rainbow.

Mnemonic devices have also become part of our everyday vocabulary in the real world and help the public remember scientific names that they otherwise would not bother to retain. Examples would be acquired immune deficiency syndrome (AIDS), severe acute respiratory syndrome (SARS), sudden infant death syndrome (SIDS), and the latest H1N1 subtype of influenza.

WHY: THEORETICAL FRAMEWORK

When appropriately used, mnemonic strategies involve higher-level thought processes since they not only assist with recall of information but with understanding of information as well. (Marzano, 2007)

Acronyms *chunk,* or connect, information together so that students don't have to recall a great deal of information simultaneously, and acronyms also help students know exactly how many items need to be remembered. (Allen, 2008a)

When students are supplied with a mnemonic device, recall and retention are improved. (Ronis, 2006)

Mnemonic strategies are time-tested techniques that enable students to remember and use material without conscious mental effort. (Mayer, 2003)

Once students have had an opportunity to completely process the information, then mnemonic devices can be used. (Marzano, 2007)

Mnemonics help the brain form a clearer memory of something, accurately encode the original information, strengthen it over time, and trigger it by a cue or an association. (Markowitz & Jensen, 2007)

Since mnemonic devices are very useful for remembering unrelated information, patterns, or rules, ordinary people can greatly improve memory performance. (Sousa, 2006)

Acrostics can be more useful to students if the content is already somewhat familiar since it provides more or less a trigger for the original information. (Allen, 2008a)

People tend to learn two- to three-times more when they use mnemonic devices than when they use their usual learning habits. (Markowitz & Jensen, 2007)

When students create their own mnemonic devices, rather than memorizing those that the teacher provides, the mnemonics are more meaningful. (Feinstein, 2009)

HOW: INSTRUCTIONAL ACTIVITIES

WHEN: During a lesson

CONTENT STANDARD(S):   All (5–12)

- Mnemonic devices are used in the real world consistently to help the public remember content that would be otherwise difficult to recall. Have students look for examples of mnemonic devices that help people remember science concepts. Some examples follow:
  o Laser: Light amplification by stimulated emission of radiation
  o Scuba: Self-contained underwater breathing apparatus
  o NASA: National Aeronautics and Space Administration
  o Radar: Radio direction and ranging
  o UFO: Unidentified flying object
  o DNA: Deoxyribonucleic acid

WHEN: During a lesson

CONTENT STANDARD(S):   All (5–12)

- Have students create their own acrostics to assist them in remembering content. For example, one teacher had students create original acrostics to remember the order of operations in math. Students will remember best what they choose to create themselves, especially if the mnemonic devices are humorous or novel.

WHEN: After a lesson

CONTENT STANDARD(S):   All (K–12)

- To assist students in recalling content previously taught and thoroughly processed, create mnemonic devices (acronyms and acrostics) that will help them remember. Teach these mnemonic devices and use them consistently during instruction, so students hear them multiple times and can use them to recall content during and after tests.

WHEN: After a lesson

CONTENT STANDARD(S):   Structure and function in living systems (5–8); Matter, energy, and organization in living systems (9–12); Systems, order, and organization (5–12)

- To help students remember the order of the classification system—kingdom, phylum, class, order, family, genus, and species—have them remember the acrostic *King Phillip Can Only Find His Green Slippers* or *King Philip Came Over For Ginger Snaps*.

WHEN: After a lesson

CONTENT STANDARD(S):   Characteristics of organisms (K–4); Structure and function in living systems (5–8); Matter, energy, and organization in living systems (9–12); Form and function (K–12)

- *"HONC if you're alive!"* would make an excellent bumper sticker! It would also assist students in remembering the four atoms most important to life: hydrogen, oxygen, nitrogen, and carbon. Since carbon is the most important atom to life, it can be circled like a copyright symbol (©). Life as we know it cannot exist without carbon.

WHEN: After a lesson

CONTENT STANDARD(S):   Structure and function in living systems (5–8); Matter, energy, and organization in living systems (9–12); Form and function (5–12)

- The 10 systems of the human body (in no particular order)—nervous, digestive, excretory, skeletal, circulatory, covering, gland, respiratory, reproductive, and muscular—can be remembered with the acrostic *Never Does Eating Some Chocolate-Covered Goodies Really Ruin Meals.*

WHEN:	After a lesson
CONTENT STANDARD(S):	Structure and function in living systems (5–8); Matter, energy, and organization in living systems (9–12); Form and function (K–12)

- The acronym GERMNRR may help students remember the following seven life functions: growth, excretion, respiration, movement, nutrition, reproduction, and response.

WHEN:	After a lesson
CONTENT STANDARD(S):	Nature of science (5–8), Nature of scientific knowledge (9–12), Abilities necessary to do scientific inquiry (5–12), Understanding about scientific inquiry (5–12), Science as human endeavor (5–12)

- Have students remember the following acrostic to help them recall the prefixes for units of the metric system from large to small: *Kids Have Dropped Over Dead Converting Metrics,* which stands for kilo, hecto, deka, ones unit, deci, centi, milli.

WHEN:	After a lesson
CONTENT STANDARD(S):	All (K–12)

- Tie a list of items you wish to remember in science with parts of your body. Think of ten things to remember; associate the first one with the top of your head, the next one with your eyes, the next one with your nose, the following one with your mouth, and continue on down the body attaching a piece of information to each body part with a vivid imaginative association. The associations will help you remember when it is time to recall the information. (Markowitz & Jensen, 2007)

WHEN:	After a lesson
CONTENT STANDARD(S):	All (K–12)

- Have students use the peg-word system and linking to remember items in order. Have them associate a rhyming word with each number 1 through 10. For example, 1 = bun, 2 = shoe, 3 = tree, 4 = door, 5 = hive, 6 = sticks, 7 = heaven, 8 = gate, 9 = sign, and 10 = hen. Have them then link each item on a list they are trying to remember with the designated rhyming word in the most absurd visual possible. If the second item on the list is *molecule,* have the student visualize the molecule in a shoe (2) to remember that *molecule* is the second thing on the list.

REFLECTION AND APPLICATION

How will I incorporate *mnemonic devices* into instruction
to engage students' brains?

Which mnemonic devices am I already incorporating into my science curriculum?

What additional devices will I incorporate?

Movement

WHAT: DEFINING THE STRATEGY

Try this movement activity to help your students remember the prefixes for units of the metric system from largest to smallest. This activity works best if you have students work in cooperative groups and take turns doing it while standing on a flight of at least seven stairs. Starting from the bottom stair up to the seventh one, place the following labels, using one on each stair: *milli, centi, deci, ones* (meters, liters, grams), *deka, hecto,* and *kilo.* Have students take turns "dancing" the steps while converting metrics. For example, have students use the problem 102.3 hectometers = ? centimeters. Have a student stand on the step labeled *hecto.* Have the student travel four steps down (or to the right) to get to the *centi* step so the answer becomes 102.3 hectometers = 1,023,000 centimeters, thereby moving the decimal point four spaces to the right. Have students notice that as they move down the stairs, or to the right, the number actually gets larger but the unit gets smaller.

Of all the 20 strategies, Strategy 10: Movement is my favorite. Why? Not only does movement help to place information in one of the strongest memory systems in the brain, procedural or muscle memory, but it makes teaching and learning so much fun! Anything that you learned while you were actively engaged, you stand a better chance of recalling. This is the reason that people seldom forget how to drive a car with a manual transmission, how to type, how to play the piano, how to ride a bicycle, or how to recall a science concept when actively engaged in learning it. In my workshops, I tell teachers that many educators have it all backward. They are going home every day exhausted, since in many classrooms teachers are doing all the work, while students are going home relaxed, since they have been the ones sitting all day. Remember that the person doing the most work is actually growing the most dendrites (brain cells).

WHY: RESEARCH RATIONALE

Physical activity in the body triggers the release of glycogen in the liver, which in the right amount, supports the formation of memories. (Jensen, E., 2009)

Dance improves attention to detail and can assist students with sequencing and thinking logically. (Karten, 2009)

Physical movement strengthens many more neurons than does lecture since lecture is a sedentary experience. (Jensen, E., 2004)

Physical performance is probably the only known cognitive activity that has been shown to use 100 percent of the brain. (Pereira et al., 2007)

When teachers ask students to retrieve handouts, materials, or equipment, change tables for discussion, or incorporate a kinesthetic aid in a science lesson, they are changing the states of students' brains. (Jensen, R., 2008)

Any task learned when we are physically engaged in doing it remains in our memory for a very long time. (Allen, 2008a)

Since physical movement increases the energy level of students, it also enhances engagement. (Marzano, 2007)

Kinesthetic engagement encapsulates information in the brain so that it can be more easily remembered and helps learners problem solve. (Jensen, E., 2004)

Students can better manage their own energy levels when they are given permission to get up, move around, stretch, or change positions. (Jensen, E., 2008)

When learners are physically engaged, more neurons are moving, feedback is provided, learners are motivated and rewarded, and emotions are accessed. (Jensen, E., 2004)

Muscle, or procedural, memory triggers the brain to produce glucose and engages more neurons than simple tasks and, therefore, strengthens memory. (Paulin, 2005)

When adolescents are involved in bodily-kinesthetic movement, the neural connections in their cerebellum are strengthened. (Feinstein, 2009)

HOW: INSTRUCTIONAL ACTIVITIES

WHEN: Before or during a lesson

CONTENT STANDARD(S):   All (K–12)

- Have students select or assign students an *energizing partner,* another student in the classroom who sits at a distance. Both students are provided with opportunities to stand and meet with one another to discuss any assigned task, such as reteaching a concept just taught by the teacher. (Gregory & Chapman, 2002)

WHEN: Before or during a lesson

CONTENT STANDARD(S):   All (5–12)

- Have students draw the *appointment clock* that follows on their paper. Put on fast-paced music and have students move around the classroom making appointments with four students in class; have them schedule an appointment with one student for twelve o'clock, a different student for three o'clock, a different one for six o'clock, and a final student for nine o'clock. Have them write each student's name on the corresponding line. Then, as you teach lessons throughout the day or week, have students keep their appointments by discussing content with one another or reteaching a concept previously taught.

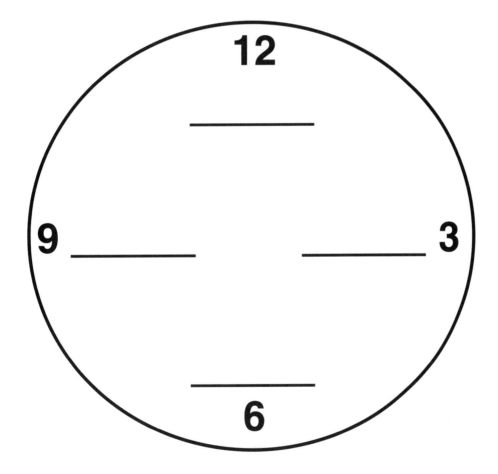

WHEN: Before or during a lesson

CONTENT STANDARD(S):   All (5–12)

- Instead of making four appointments on the clock, use *element buddies.* Have students label their clocks with the first 12 elements of the periodic table. Have them put a line next to each element. As lessons are taught throughout the week, have student make appointments with 12 of their peers whose names have been written on the lines next to each element.

WHEN:	During a lesson
CONTENT STANDARD(S):	All (K–12)

- Rather than having students always raise their hands if they agree with an answer provided by a classmate, have them stand if they agree and remain seated if they disagree. Standing provides more blood and oxygen throughout the body and keeps your students more alert.

WHEN:	During a lesson
CONTENT STANDARD(S):	All (5–12)

- Have students take a *carousel gallery walk* by setting up four stations or easels in the room. Write a different question or idea to comment about on each easel. Have students form four groups and rotate to each station answering the questions or commenting on the ideas on each easel. Playing high-energy music while this activity proceeds will add to its appeal.

WHEN:	During a lesson
CONTENT STANDARD(S):	Abilities necessary to do scientific inquiry (K–12), Understanding about scientific inquiry (K–12), Science as human endeavor (K–12)

- Set up several mini-experiments or observations around the room. Have students form as many groups as there are experiments, and have them move every 10 minutes to the next station. Students read each set of directions and record their answers at each station. This activity can be used with a variety of concepts such as systems of the human body, field tests, or weather stations.

WHEN:	During a lesson
CONTENT STANDARD(S):	Properties and changes of properties in matter (5–8), Structure and properties of matter (9–12), Chemical reactions (9–12)

- Have students create T-shirts for individual elements in the periodic table or make cards for the elements. Have them arrange themselves into a periodic table. They can also combine into molecules by moving toward one another.

WHEN:	During a lesson
CONTENT STANDARD(S):	Changes in earth and sky (K–4), Earth in the solar system (5–8), Origin and evolution of the earth system (9–12)

- Have students *become* the earth. Have them stand up and tilt 23.5 degrees while rotating and revolving around another student who is simulating the sun. In this way, they can learn about how days, years, and seasons are created.

WHEN:	During a lesson
CONTENT STANDARD(S):	Characteristics of organisms (K–4); Structure and function in living systems (5–8); Interdependence of organisms (9–12); Matter, energy, and organization in living systems (9–12)

- Give students cards with the words *kingdom, phylum, class, order, family, genus,* and *species* on them. Then, have seven students with cards arrange themselves into the classification system in order. This activity can be used in conjunction with Warren Phillips's song "Classification" (the classification song can be found on iTunes or on the CDs that are available for purchase at www.wphillips.com). Have them hold up their cards as they sing. Other cards can be added with vocabulary from the song.

WHEN:	During a lesson
CONTENT STANDARD(S):	Organisms and environments (K–4), Populations and ecosystems (5–8), Interdependence of organisms (9–12), Evolution and equilibrium (K–12)

- Have students create a food web using string. Give each student the name of an animal or insect in the food chain. Have them sit in a circle and pass the string to elements of the food chain that they depend on. A web is created. See what happens when you cut the string and one part of the food web disappears.

WHEN:	During a lesson
CONTENT STANDARD(S):	Position and motion of objects (K–4), Properties and changes of properties in matter (5–8), Motions and forces (5–12), Transfer of energy (5–8), Interactions of energy and matter (9–12)

- Have students simulate atom movement by shaking their fists. This shaking represents the fact that all atoms vibrate and have energy.

Two atoms shaking are done with two fists. If the fists are maintaining relative position, they are simulating a solid. If the fists are rotating around one another, they are simulating a liquid. A gas would be simulated by taking the fists and extending them out far away from one another. Plasma would be simulated when the arms are moving wildly and the fists are opening to extend the fingers, implying that light is released. These movements can accompany the song "The States of Matter" found in Strategy 11 of this book.

WHEN: During a lesson

CONTENT STANDARD(S):   Characteristics of organisms (K–4), Structure and function in living systems (5–8), Behavior of organisms (9–12), Understanding about scientific inquiry (K–12)

- Have students participate in *cricket jumping.* Have them jump three times and then take the average of the three jumps. Have students compare their jumps to those of crickets. Have them compare human and cricket body weights to the distances jumped as a ratio. This activity is good for graphing practice.

WHEN: During a lesson

CONTENT STANDARD(S):   Abilities necessary to do scientific inquiry (5–12), Understanding about scientific inquiry (5–12)

- Place 10 baskets, numbered 1 through 10, in the front of the room. The same five questions are placed in five envelopes in each basket. Randomly assign each student a basket number. Students get up from their seats and come to the front of the room to get a question from their assigned basket. They then answer the question in writing back at their seats, bring the envelope back, and place it into the basket. Have them then get a different envelope from the same basket until they have answered all of the questions. This activity is usually done quietly as a quiz.

REFLECTION AND APPLICATION

How will I incorporate *movement* into instruction to engage students' brains?

Which movement activities am I already incorporating into my science curriculum?

What additional activities will I incorporate?

Strategy 11

Music, Rhythm, Rhyme, and Rap

WHAT: DEFINING THE STRATEGY

The true story is told of Douglas Hegdahl, an American POW, who was captured by the Vietcong during the Vietnam War. Since he was going to be released eventually, Douglas was asked to remember the names of as many other POWs as possible, so their families could be notified. When released, Douglas sang the names of over 200 prisoners to the tune of "Old MacDonald Had a Farm." Had he not been able to sing the names, it is hardly likely that he would have remembered so many.

Seven years ago, I had the privilege of meeting one of the best teachers in the country. His name is Warren Phillips, and he uses many of the 20 brain-compatible strategies to engage his middle school students. In fact, I was so impressed with his ability to teach science that I asked if he would coauthor this book. One of his favorite strategies is music. He has taken the science standards and written songs that help all students remember the major concepts. Those songs are recorded in a *Sing-A-Long Science* series that can be found on his website at www.wphillips.com. The tunes are familiar, but the lyrics are original. Many of Warren's students return years later and thank him for his songs, which they not only never forget but also continue to use to retain science concepts and increase test performance. The following quote expresses the feelings of one of Warren's students:

Hey Mr. P!

I just want to thank you for teaching us the sing-along-science songs! Today, I took the SAT II Biology—E and many of your songs (such as Classification, The Scientific Method Song, and DNA) helped me ace many sections of it. Again, thank you for your boundless creativity!

—Marina R.

Music changes the state of the brain, but it also helps students remember. Several of Warren Phillips's songs are included in the instructional activities section of this chapter.

WHY: THEORETICAL FRAMEWORK

Teachers should match the music to the instructional task. For example, play baroque, classical, or mellow New Age for seat work or discussion; classic rhythm and blues or oldies for fun sing-alongs; high-tempo vocals for activities that do not require talking; high-tempo instrumental when students are moving; or themes from TV or game shows when appropriate. (Jensen, E., 2009)

When information is tied to music, it stands a better chance of being encoded into long-term memory. (Jensen, E., 2008)

Background sounds or music while learning, songs with lyrics that relate to content, sounds from the environment, or even tapping to the learning all foster the students' musical-rhythmic intelligence. (Karten, 2007)

Every country in the world with the highest math and science results also has strong music and arts programs. (Jensen, E., 2008)

Music is one of the most powerful tools for changing the states of students since it can set a mood in class, help students to focus, get and hold their attention, and make your classroom a much more comfortable place to be. (Jensen, R., 2008)

Almost every one of the high school students who have previously won the Siemens Competition in Math, Science, and Technology plays one or more musical instruments. (Jensen, E., 2008)

Music has the ability to energize or relax students, develop rapport with them, establish the tone for the day, invigorate their minds, encourage fun, and provide inspiration. (Jensen, E., 2009)

Since it is tied to the emotional and spatial intelligences and connected to sequential and logical skills as well, musical intelligence does not reside in one place in the brain. (Kagan & Kagan, 2007)

Classical music by composers like Beethoven and Mozart is appropriate for students to use when brainstorming or problem solving since it stimulates beta waves in the brain. (Sprenger, 2007)

According to studies of musicians, when certain areas of the auditory cortex are meaningfully stimulated, the mass of the brain in the auditory area increases. (Jensen, E., 2004)

The brain appears to be specialized for music since the auditory cortex responds to tones and pitch and brain cells process the contour of the melody. (Weinberger, 2004)

The critical ingredient for improving the performance of students on spatial tasks is musical rhythm. (Jensen, E., 2004)

Change the music during a learning episode: Set an emotional mood before class starts; then use upbeat tunes for moving around the room and music appropriate to the task during seat work; end the class with positive music. (Sousa, 2006)

Song incorporates the elements of melody, harmony, tone, and rhythm for the purpose of inserting emotion into a verbal message, which is now slowed down. (Sylwester, 2003)

HOW: INSTRUCTIONAL ACTIVITIES

WHEN: Before or after a lesson

CONTENT STANDARD(S):   All (5–12)

- Put your creative talents to work! Write an original song, rhyme, or rap to symbolize your understanding of a concept you previously taught the class. Perform your creative effort for your students, and teach it to them so that they can use the powerful effects of music to remember your content. They'll love you for it!

WHEN: Before, during, or after a lesson

CONTENT STANDARD(S):   All (K–12)

- Music can change the state of students' brains. Consult books that can assist you with your selection of music such as Eric Jensen's (2005) *Top Tunes for Teaching* or Rich Allen's (2008b) *The Ultimate Book of Music for Learning*. The second edition of my book *Worksheets Don't Grow Dendrites: 20 Instructional Strategies That Engage the Brain* also contains a list of some of my favorite artists and the CDs that I use when teaching students and adults.

WHEN: Before, during, or after a lesson

CONTENT STANDARD(S):   Matter, energy, and organization in living systems (9–12); Structure and function in living systems (5–8); Form and function (5–12)

- Have students sing the following song to recall information about the brain:

The Brain Song

(Sung to the tune of "When Johnny Comes Marching Home Again")

A hundred billion neurons make a human brain

Connecting and communicating in a chain

From cells with axons that neurotransmit

Throughout your body—lickety split

And the cer-e-bell-um keeps them closely knit

The cere-brum is the largest part with lots of folds

Divided into hemispheres—and they control

Intelligence, person-ality too

Motor functions and senses that you

Need to con-scious-ly determine what to do

The frontal lobe controls your judgment and your moves

The parietal lobe has senses all within the grooves

The occipital lobe—sight and reading is there

The temporal—memory and what you hear

And the cor-pus callo-sum connects the hemispheres

Pituitary glands make hormones and release

Them when you're growing older and your needs increase

The hypo-thal-amus keeps you warm

The brain stem with precision informs

Your in-vol-un-tar-y muscles to perform

An almond-sized a-myg-da-la holds memories

Connected with emotions that will guarantee

You'll remember the smells and the sights and the sounds

Of special moments that come around

'Cause emo-tional learning is the most profound!

Source: Copyright Warren Phillips, 2007. Used with permission.

WHEN:	Before, during, or after a lesson
CONTENT STANDARD(S):	Characteristics of organisms (K–4); Structure and function in living systems (5–8); Matter, energy, and organization in living systems ((9–12); Systems, order, and organization (K–12); Evidence, models, and explanation (K–12); Form and function (K–12)

S-K-I-N

(A parody sung to the tune of "YMCA")

Verse 1

You there! Tanning skin in the sun!

Epidermis, damage may have begun

That top layer helps protect us from harm

Like bacteria and bad germs

Your skin is shedding from head to toe

While it's making many new cells below

Plus the pigment, melanin is displayed

It protects us from U-V rays!

Chorus

I'm all wrapped up in my S-K-I-N

I'm all wrapped up in my S-K-I-N

It makes vitamin D, keeps your body waste free

Stops infections from getting to me!

Verse 2

Derm-is, the second layer of skin

With blood vessels all around us within

And nerve endings let us feel what's out there

While the foll-i-cles grow our hair

Oil glands, there is sebum produced

Keeps our skin moist, and our skin waterproof

And the sweat glands, sweat comes out of our pores

To help us maintain temperatures!

Chorus

I'm all wrapped up in my S-K-I-N

I'm all wrapped up in my S-K-I-N

It makes vitamin D, keeps your body waste free

Stops infections from getting to me!

Verse 3

Bottom sub-cu-ta-ne-ous skin

Mostly fatty so it holds the heat in

Shock absorbing—when you bump and you bruise

And it holds—skin-to our tissues!

Chorus

I'm all wrapped up in my S-K-I-N

I'm all wrapped up in my S-K-I-N

It makes vitamin D, keeps your body waste free

Stops infections from getting to me!

Source: From *Sing-A-Long Science, The Second Sequel.* Copyright Warren Phillips and Matt Fisher, 2003. Used with permission.

Using your body and arms, make the letters *S, K, I,* and *N* to add to the fun and procedural memory in the hippocampus (Warren Phillips has had different classes use slightly different motions for each letter).

WHEN: Before, during, or after a lesson

CONTENT STANDARD(S):   Light, heat, electricity, and magnetism (K–4); Transfer of energy (5–8); Interactions of energy and matter (9–12); Form and function (5–12)

The Optics Song

Image by
Animation
Factory.

(A parody sung to the tune of "Head, Shoulders, Knees, and Toes")

The sunlight shines on where we live (where we live!)

The spectrum's made of ROY G. BIV (ROY G. BIV!)

Red, Orange, Yellow, and Green and Blue

Indigo and Vi-o-let (Violet!)

Light Rays travel in straight lines (in straight lines!)

And it happens all the time (all the time!)

And when it hits a different medium

It refracts and it bends some (it bends some!)

Convex lenses focus light (focus light!)

What was "left" before is "right" (now it's right!)

Beyond the focal point, the image flips

And the image also tips (also tips!)

Concave lenses scatter light (scatter light!)

The scattered image isn't bright (isn't bright!)

It's blurry and the rays all move away

Refraction makes them fade away (fade away!)

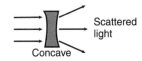

Image by
Animation
Factory.

Image by
Animation
Factory.

Source: From *Sing-A-Long Science.* Copyright Warren Phillips, 1999. Used with permission.

WHEN:	Before, during, or after a lesson
CONTENT STANDARD(S):	Position and motion of objects (K–4), Properties and changes of properties in matter (5–8), Transfer of energy (5–8), Motions and forces (5–12), Interactions of energy and matter (9–12), Conservation of energy and increase in disorder (9–12)

The States of Matter

(A parody sung to the tune of "Battle Hymn of the Republic")

Verse 1

The states of matter come from atoms energy they store

And it's constantly exerted as they vibrate back and forth

As the energy accumulates, the atoms vibrate more

Phase changes can occur!

Image by
Animation
Factory.

Chorus

Solid, Liquid, Gas and Plasma

Solid, Liquid, Gas and Plasma

Solid, Liquid, Gas and Plasma

And now Bose-Einstein!

Verse 2

Solids have less energy with atoms locked in place

Liquid atoms move around and take up different shapes

Gaseous atoms move apart and fill up any space

And Plasma photons glow!

Chorus

Solid, Liquid, Gas and Plasma

Solid, Liquid, Gas and Plasma

Solid, Liquid, Gas and Plasma

And now Bose-Einstein!

Image by
Animation
Factory.

Verse 3

Now Einstein hypothesized another state exists

And more recently a scientist has found what he had missed

A state at real cold temperatures that aren't in our midst

Bose found it could subsist!

Chorus

Solid, Liquid, Gas and Plasma

Solid, Liquid, Gas and Plasma

Solid, Liquid, Gas and Plasma

And now Bose-Einstein!

And now Bose-Einstein!

And now Bose-Einstein!

Source: From *Sing-A-Long Science, The Sequel.* Copyright Warren Phillips, 2002. Used with permission.

There are hand movements, which represent atomic movement in different states of matter, that add to the procedural memory in the hippocampus—and to the fun. They include clapping (Bose-Einstein); two fists wiggling (solids); two fists rotating (liquids); two arms outstretched with fists (gas); and two arms outstretched, fingers opening and closing (plasma).

WHEN:	Before, during, or after a lesson
CONTENT STANDARD(S):	All (K–12)

- Play calming music as students enter your science classroom. Music within the range of 50 to 70 beats per minute lines up with the heart and calms down students' brains. Types of music with this range include classical, jazz, Celtic, New Age, Native American, and nature sounds. I have a wonderful CD of music I bought from the aquarium in Sydney, Australia. The calming sounds of the water bring an immediate tranquility to students' brains. Calming music can also be played when students are involved in lab work or scientific investigations.

WHEN:	Before, during, or after a lesson
CONTENT STANDARD(S):	All (K–12)

- Sometimes you do not want your students calm. Sometimes you want them energized, such as when they are simulating molecules in a gas. If this is the case, play songs within a tempo range of 110 to 160 beats per minute. This high-energy music not only creates excitement and enthusiasm but also goes a long way in making your lesson memorable. Types of music that fall into this category include salsa, rhythm and blues (R&B), rock and roll, and fast-paced country.

WHEN:	During a lesson
CONTENT STANDARD(S):	All (K–12)

- Remember not to play music when you are directly instructing your students. It can be disturbing to some students when they have to decide whether to listen to you or to the music. If you use music during lab work, keep the volume low so as not to disrupt the thought processes of your students.

WHEN:	After a lesson
CONTENT STANDARD(S):	Motions and forces (9–12), Interactions of energy and matter (9–12), Conservation of energy and increase in disorder (9–12), Form and function (5–12)

- To remember physical laws that deal with gases, have students try the following rhymes:

Charles's law states that for a constant volume, pressure is directly proportional to temperature. Rhyme: *If the tank's too hot, Chuck, you're blown into muck.*

Henry's law states that the solubility of a gas increases with pressure. Rhyme: *To remember good old Hank, remember the bubbles in the Coke you drank.*

Boyle's law states that at constant temperature, pressure is inversely proportional to volume. Rhyme: *Boyle's law is best of all because it presses gases awfully small.*

WHEN: After a lesson

CONTENT STANDARDS(S):   All (K–12)

- To assist students in recalling information following a lesson, have them walk, march, or dance around the room to high-energy, fast-paced music. Periodically stop the music and have students form groups of three or four standing in close proximity. Have them recall a major concept covered in the lesson and discuss it with their respective groups. Then, start the music again and have them walk in a different direction so that when they stop, they are not standing next to the same students. Have them repeat the procedure with another group and a second major concept.

WHEN: After a lesson

CONTENT STANDARD(S):   All (5–12)

- Have students work in cooperative groups to write a cinquain that symbolizes their understanding of a concept previously taught or content read. The format of a cinquain is as follows: first line—one word, second line—two words, third line—three words, fourth line—four words, last line—one word.

Example

Brain

Social organism

Thinking, linking, connecting

Necessary for life itself

Life

(Tate, 2010, p. 83)

WHEN: After a lesson

CONTENT STANDARD(S):   All (5–12)

- Following instruction in a major concept, have students write an original song, rhyme, or rap to symbolize their understanding of the concept taught. Students can be assigned this task for homework, if class time does not permit. Then on the following day, all students can attend a talent show where volunteers pretend to be on *American Idol* and get up and perform their original effort for the class. What a fun way to review content! (Tate, 2010)

REFLECTION AND APPLICATION

> How will I incorporate *music, rhythm, rhyme,* and *rap* into instruction to engage students' brains?

Which music, rhythm, rhyme, and rap activities am I already incorporating into my science curriculum?

What additional activities will I incorporate?

Strategy 12

Project-Based and Problem-Based Instruction

WHAT: DEFINING THE STRATEGY

Warren Phillips, master science teacher, song-writer, and co-author of this book, not only used his original song lyrics to get students excited about science and to help them retain concepts, he also used project-based instruction as his main method of delivering instruction. Students in Warren's class participated in a program called HOWL, which is an acronym for *Helping Others While Learning*. This exceptional methodology encouraged students to master their curricula objectives while participating in interdisciplinary projects that provided a service to the school and community. An example of a HOWL project follows.

Students were charged with the responsibility of working with other teachers in the building to design a Jeopardy game, which the receiving teacher would then use with students to review content. A rubric was developed outlining specifically what the Jeopardy game should look like and include. Students' games received three evaluations based on the rubric: one from Mr. Phillips, one from the receiving teacher, and a personal one from the student.

When I taught students to problem solve, I didn't start with the problems in the textbook. Who cares about Tommy and Sue in the textbook? Actually, no one! I made up real-life problems; and I put the names of students in the class in the problems, so they saw themselves solving the problems. This technique placed students' brains closer to the reason they exist in the first place, to solve problems in the real world.

WHY: THEORETICAL FRAMEWORK

Problem solving, creativity, and critical thinking have a tendency to be neglected on nationwide tests in favor of facts and procedures—the very tasks the national science standards sought to change. (Berns & Sandler, 2009)

Community recycling or beautification projects, as well as organized environments at home and school, enable students to use their naturalist intelligence. (Karten, 2007)

When students are able to apply the learning to their personal lives and understand the relationship between school success and real-world success, engagement increases and they feel more responsibility for completing school assignments. (Algozzine, Campbell, & Wang, 2009b)

Projects enable students to explore concepts like real-world investigators and researchers and to create novel products through which they show their conceptual understanding. (Hammerman, 2009)

Problem-based learning projects and service-learning opportunities help teachers structure student interaction in a brain-compatible classroom. (Fogarty, 2009)

The most benefit is gained when projects enable students to make personal connections that draw them into the learning. (Karten, 2007)

Problem solving to the brain is what aerobic exercise is to the body since solving challenging, novel, complex problems creates a flourish of neural activity. Synapses form, blood flow accelerates, and neurotransmitters become active. (Jensen, E., 2008)

Parallel processing happens in the brain when a student is engaged in making decisions or solving problems. (Fogarty, 2001)

The challenge of a problem engages the intellect of the brain since the brain tries to make sense of the dissonance it is experiencing while solving the problem. (Fogarty, 2009)

Students are intensely interested in projects since they are able to engage in "digging in, messing around, and figuring things out." (Fogarty, 2009, p. 154)

Complex problems necessitate complex brain activity. (Fogarty, 2009)

Movement strengthens the cerebellum, which is essential for efficient problem-solving skills and planning. (Feinstein, 2009)

Students' learning increased when they were actively involved in thematic projects that were long term, involved enriched language, and incorporated alternative forms of assessment. (Pinkerton, 1994)

HOW: INSTRUCTIONAL ACTIVITIES

WHEN: During a lesson

CONTENT STANDARD(S):   Science as a human endeavor (K–4), Nature of science (5–8), History of science (5–8), Nature of scientific knowledge (9–12), Historical perspectives (9–12)

- Have students create a time line of important scientific discoveries. Each student can work on one discovery, and the entire class can assemble the time line when finished. Have younger students draw the discoveries rather than write them.

WHEN: During a lesson

CONTENT STANDARD(S):   Earth in the solar system (5–8), Origin and evolution of the universe (9–12), Abilities of technological design (9–12)

- Have the class make a model of the solar system while figuring the ratio of size to distances. This model can be displayed in the halls of the school, stretching from one end to the other. It will also show the vast *nothingness* of our solar system. Using the same scale, students can also figure the distance to the nearest star, which is incredibly far.

WHEN: During a lesson

CONTENT STANDARD(S):   Historical perspectives (9–12); Change, constancy, and measurement (K–12); Evolution and equilibrium (K–12); Origin and evolution of the universe (9–12)

- Have students create a time line that shows a geologic history of life. One meter being equal to one million years works well in most classrooms. This scale will show the vast amounts of time with no advanced life. It will also show the brief time that humans have existed on earth and the relative success of sustained life for the dinosaurs. Have younger students draw rather than write out the events.

WHEN: During a lesson

CONTENT STANDARD(S):   Evidence, models, and explanation (K–12); Science as a human endeavor (K–12); Understanding about scientific inquiry (K–12)

- Have students create a museum right in your classroom. Put students in cooperative groups. Put each group in charge of an *exhibit*. Have students distribute tickets so that students in other classrooms can visit the museum as they conduct tours of their exhibits.

WHEN: During or after a lesson

CONTENT STANDARD(S):   Regulation and behavior (5–8); The cell (9–12); Populations, resources, and environments (5–8); Environmental quality (9–12)

- This project uses the strategy of metaphor to compare a raw egg to a cell. First measure the circumference around the top, bottom and middle of the egg or the egg's *north* and *south* poles and *equator*. Continue to record these numbers each day.
  - Day 1: Put the egg in vinegar.
  - Day 2: Rinse off the egg and place it back into vinegar.
  - Day 3: The shell will be dissolved, exposing the cell membrane. Place the egg into water with food coloring.
  - Day 4: The egg will have absorbed the food coloring into the membrane by osmosis, the very same way that food enters a cell. Place the egg into saltwater (use a saturated salt solution). Add salt until it no longer dissolves but accumulates in the water.
  - Day 5: The egg will have gotten much smaller and the food coloring will have been pulled out of the egg by osmosis (similar to what happens when we drink saltwater and become dehydrated due to the osmosis).
  - Days 6 through 10: Place the egg on a paper towel. It will shrivel each day. Since it has salt in it, the egg will stay preserved as it dries and can be kept for years.

This can be a great two-week project that students can do at home. They can name the egg, and some students actually become attached to it. Have them save the egg when they are done with the project and bring it to school for bonus points. A graph of the egg's daily measurements and journal entries can accompany the final project grade.

WHEN: During a lesson

CONTENT STANDARD(S):   Properties and changes of properties in matter (5–8), Interactions of energy and matter (9–12)

- Have students build bridges out of gumdrops, peas soaked in vinegar, toothpicks, or pasta (linguine and fettuccine). Students build a budget and "pay" for their supplies. Bridges are tested at the end of the bridge building with a strength test by placing various weights, such as books, on the bridge to see which bridge is the strongest. Warren Phillips has a song about *bridges* in his *Sing-A-Long Science* series, which can accompany this project. Go to his website at www.wphillips.com.

WHEN: During a lesson

CONTENT STANDARD(S):   Motions and forces (5–12), Conservation of energy and increase in disorder (9–12), Interactions of energy and matter (9–12)

- Have students design and launch two-liter bottle rockets. An adapter can be used to hold the rockets in place. These can be made yourself (see www.instructables.com/id/Soda-Bottle-Rocket) or purchased (see www.arborsci.com). Place a little water in the bottle and pump in air. When released, the bottle will go up about 100 feet into the air. Students can use a glue gun to attach fins and cones to their rockets. They can also paint them with poster paints prior to launching. Advanced classes can measure the angle and distance to determine the height of the rocket.

WHEN:	During a lesson
CONTENT STANDARD(S):	Abilities necessary to do scientific inquiry (5–12); Understanding about scientific inquiry (5–12); Structure and function in living systems (5–8); Diversity and adaptations of organisms (5–8); Matter, energy, and organization in living systems (9–12)

- Put students in cooperative groups. Give each group a pumpkin. Have them count the number of ribs, weigh the pumpkin in grams, measure the pumpkin's circumference, and estimate the number of seeds the pumpkin contains. They can then turn their pumpkin into a jack-o'-lantern and weigh the cut-out parts. Students can also figure out the volume of the pumpkin's "guts" and draw cross-section, lateral, and dorsal views of it. This project can be followed up with additional pumpkin research and works well in keeping with the holidays.

WHEN:	During a lesson
CONTENT STANDARD(S):	Characteristics and changes in populations (K–4); Populations, resources, and environments (5–8); Natural resources (9–12); Change, constancy, and measurement (K–12)

- Create a garden outside of the school. This could be a vegetable or a flower garden. The school logo, color, and initials could be grown in flowers. A nature garden is another good idea. Have students label plants with scientific names and conduct tours. Warren's class made a water garden next to a window in the cafeteria of his school so that all students could see the fish and observe changes every day.

WHEN:	During a lesson
CONTENT STANDARD(S):	Structure and function in living systems (5–8); Diversity and adaptations of organisms (5–8); Matter, energy, and organization in living systems (9–12)

- Put students in cooperative groups of four to six. Have each group create a field guide of one local plant or animal, which can be used before a field trip or at the field trip itself.

WHEN:	During a lesson
CONTENT STANDARD(S):	Properties of objects and materials (K–4), Risks and benefits (5–8), Structure and properties of matter (9–12), Environmental quality (9–12), Natural and human-induced hazards (9–12)

- Find some biodegradable packing peanuts. You can often find these in the packing of materials that you have bought, but they are also available at www.uline.com. These packing peanuts look like regular styrofoam ones; but they are actually made of cornstarch and, therefore, biodegrade when placed in water. Varying the temperature of the water affects the rate at which they dissolve. Divide students into groups, with each group testing a different water temperature. This is a good project regarding recycling and is also good for teaching graphing.

WHEN:	During or after a lesson
CONTENT STANDARD(S):	Abilities necessary to do scientific inquiry (5–12), Understanding about scientific inquiry (5–12), Science as human endeavor (5–12)

- Engage students in a project in which they research how the content taught in school is used in real-world professions. For example, have them research how scientists use science concepts, and so forth.

WHEN:	After a lesson
CONTENT STANDARD(S):	Organisms and environments (K–4), Populations and ecosystems (5–8), Diversity and adaptations of organisms (5–8), Biological evolution (9–12), Interdependence of organisms (9–12)

- Have students create a rainforest or other ecosystem in the classroom or in another designated area in the school. Have them label the plants and animals with scientific names and provide information sheets on each plant and animal. Have students give tours to the rest of the school. Warren Phillips's seventh-grade class actually created a rainforest, and he has pictures to prove it!

WHEN:	After a lesson
CONTENT STANDARD(S):	Structure and function in living systems (5–8), The cell (9–12), Molecular basis of heredity (9–12)

- To help them recall the parts of an animal cell, have students complete a homework assignment. Have them make a pizza that displays their knowledge of the parts of the cell. Students will decide what toppings will be used to replicate parts of the cell, such as pepperoni for the nucleus. On a designated day, have students bring their pizzas to school and evaluate one another's pizzas based on a rubric they helped to develop. Following the evaluation, be sure the class eats their pizzas and enjoys a "cellebration"!

REFLECTION AND APPLICATION

How will I incorporate *project-based* and *problem-based instruction* to engage students' brains?

Which project-based and problem-based activities am I already incorporating into my science curriculum?

What additional activities will I incorporate?

Reciprocal Teaching and Cooperative Learning

WHAT: DEFINING THE STRATEGY

When I was taught to be a teacher over 35 years ago, if two students in my class were talking about the content I was teaching, they were accused of cheating. Now the brain research is telling us that the one doing the most talking in class is actually growing the most *dendrites* (brain cells). In many classrooms I observe, that person is the teacher. We have a large number of teachers who are so smart since they are growing dendrites on a daily basis! Students have got to be a part of the conversation. In fact, students learn at least 90% of what they teach to others (Society for Developmental Education, 1995; Sousa, 2006).

The next time you have a great deal of science text to get through, divide the text into sections, place your students in heterogeneous groups, and assign one section of the text to one person in each group. That person's job is to become an expert on their particular section so that they can eventually teach it to their group. An intermediate step would be to have students meet with students in other groups who have the same part so that they can plan the presentation together. Have them then return to their original group and teach. Give students the option of being creative in the way they teach the content. They can make visuals, have students involved in a role play, write a song or rap to get the information across, or use any additional brain-compatible strategy. Students are not allowed to read the information aloud to their group. That's too boring! Sit back and watch how imaginative students can be when they are permitted to *jigsaw* the material. When only one student has a piece of the puzzle, it takes the entire group to complete it. Be sure to conduct a whole-class review of the most pertinent facts so that every student hears the information at least twice.

WHY: THEORETICAL FRAMEWORK

Cooperative-learning strategies make thinking and learning audible. (Fogarty, 2009)

Understanding and thinking are fostered by both the listener and the learner during the conversation and questions and answers that take place when students are involved in cooperative-group learning. (Fogarty, 2009)

It is a teacher's job to ensure that all students develop the set of social skills essential for interacting productively with other students since our very survival as humans depends on relationships. (Jensen, E., 2008)

Cooperative learning is one of nine instructional strategies most likely to improve academic achievement regardless of the content area or grade level. (Mangan, 2007)

Cooperative-learning activities teach students to work with other students in teams, a prerequisite for successful living in the twenty-first century. (Mangan, 2007)

Guided reciprocal peer questioning is a procedure in which students in small groups question one another about the content using open-ended, higher-order question stems that foster thinking and generate discussion. (Keeley, 2008, p. 106)

Having students work in groups not only allows students time to teach and learn from one another, but it helps them realize how much content knowledge they actually have acquired and gives them feedback on their performance. (Jensen, E., 2004)

Cooperative-learning groups will assist in scaffolding students' higher-order thinking skills and tap into their multiple intelligences. (Caine, Caine, McClintic, & Klimek, 2005)

One of the 10 things that every child needs to build strong emotional intelligence is the ability to interact with others in their environment. (McCormick Tribune Foundation, 1999)

When humans work collaboratively, thinking is elicited that is far superior to individual effort since people are social beings. (Costa, 2008)

When students talk with each other, they have the chance to release pent-up energy as well as state their thoughts, opinions, and feelings. (Allen, 2008a)

Having students work in cooperative groups enables them to teach and learn from one another. This assists them in figuring out how much content knowledge they already have and provides them with informal feedback related to their performance. (Jensen, E., 2004)

HOW: INSTRUCTIONAL ACTIVITIES

WHEN: Before a lesson

CONTENT STANDARD(S):   All (K–12)

- Have students draw the face of a clock. Have them write the numbers *12, 3, 6,* and *9* in the appropriate places on the clock. Have students draw one line near each number. This clock becomes their vehicle for making appointments with their peers in class. Put on some fast-paced music and have students walk around the classroom and make appointments with four different students in class. They should write the name of the person they made each appointment with on the line next to the number so that later in the class, when it is time to meet with their appointment, they can remember with whom they made the appointment. See Strategy 10: Movement for a sample of the appointment clock.

  Stop periodically throughout the period or the day and have students keep their appointments. Appointments can be used to reteach a concept previously taught or to discuss an open-ended question pertaining to the lesson. (Tate, 2010)

WHEN: Before, during, or after a lesson

CONTENT STANDARD(S):   All (K–12)

- Have each student select a close partner (CP) or an elbow partner who sits so close to the student that they can talk with this person without getting out of their seat. The job of this partner is to periodically reteach science content previously taught or to discuss an open-ended question assigned by the teacher. The close-partner technique takes very little time but can be invaluable in helping students retain and understand content.

WHEN: During a lesson

CONTENT STANDARD(S):   All (5–12)

- Jigsaw is a great cooperative-learning technique when dealing with a large amount of content. In this activity, students become "experts" on one part of the information, by reading the text, taking notes, and so forth. After time is given for the experts to learn their material, groups are made, consisting of one expert from each section. The experts must then teach their information to the rest of their group. For example, when learning about the layers of the atmosphere, the class is divided into five groups. Group 1 investigates the troposphere; Group 2, the stratosphere; Group 3, the mesosphere; Group 4, the thermosphere; and Group 5, the exosphere. After a set amount of time to prepare to teach, the class is then divided into groups consisting of one expert from each of the layers. When the group meets, the troposphere expert teaches everyone about that layer, and so forth, until all group members have taught. It becomes the teacher's responsibility to review each of the earth's layers with the entire class to ensure that every student is given the most important points in the information. In addition, each student gets to hear it twice: once from a peer and once from the teacher.

WHEN: During a lesson

CONTENT STANDARD(S):   All (K–12)

- Have students work together in cooperative groups, or families, of four to six students. They may be seated in groups already or taught to pick up their desks and arrange them into groups for a cooperative-learning activity and to put them back once the activity is over. It is recommended that the groups be of mixed-ability levels to capitalize on the various multiple intelligences or talents of students.

  Give each group the same task. Have them discuss the thought processes involved in completing the task and reach consensus as to the correct answer. Once the answer is agreed upon, have each person in the group sign the paper that the answer is written on, verifying that they agree with the answer and, if called upon randomly, could explain how the solution was derived to the entire class. This individual accountability helps to ensure that one person does not do all the work while other students watch their efforts. (Tate, 2010)

WHEN: During a lesson

CONTENT STANDARD(S):   All (5–12)

- When students have difficulty working together as a cooperative group, you may want to teach some social skills necessary for effective functioning. For example, construct a T-chart similar to the one that follows where each social skill is considered from two perspectives: *what it looks like* and *what it sounds like*. Have students brainstorm ideas for what the social skill would look like or sound like. Social skills could include the following: paying undivided attention, encouraging one another, or critiquing ideas and not peers.

Encouraging

Looks Like	Sounds Like
Heads nodding	Way to go!
One person speaking	Good job!
Smiles	Good idea!
Eye contact	What do you think?

- Observe each group and make a tally mark on a sheet each time the social skill is practiced by any student in the group. Provide feedback to the class during a debriefing following the cooperative activity. You may also assign a student in each group to fulfill the function of a *process observer* who collects the data for the group.

WHEN:	During a lesson
CONTENT STANDARD(S):	Characteristics of organisms (K–4); Structure and function in living systems (5–8); The cell (9–12); Evidence, models, and explanation (K–12); Form and function (K–12)

- Teach one-half of the class what they need to know about animal cells. Teach the other half about plant cells. Students are then required to partner with a student from the opposite half of the class and teach what they learned about either plant or animal cells to their partners. Students can then use a graphic organizer, called a *Venn diagram,* to compare and contrast what they have learned about both types of cells.

Compare/Contrast

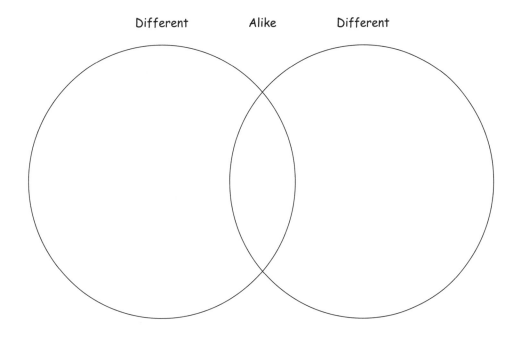

Different   Alike   Different

WHEN: During a lesson

CONTENT STANDARD(S):   All (5–12)

- Another way to help ensure individual accountability is to assign group roles for students to fulfill during the cooperative-learning activity. Some of the following roles can be assigned:
  o **Facilitator:** Ensures that the group stays on task and completes the assigned activity
  o **Scribe:** Writes down anything the group has to submit in writing
  o **Timekeeper:** Tells the group when half the time is over and when there is one minute remaining
  o **Reporter:** Gives an oral presentation to the class regarding the results of the group's work
  o **Materials Manager:** Collects any materials or other resources that the group needs to complete the task
  o **Process Observer:** Provides feedback to the group on how well they practiced their social skills during the cooperative-learning activity (Tate, 2010, p. 95)

WHEN: During a lesson

CONTENT STANDARD(S):   Abilities of technological design (K–12), Understanding about science and technology (K–12), Abilities necessary to do scientific inquiry (K–12)

- To address the *communication strand* in the science curriculum, have students work together in each science class to create a special code and a transcription key. Have students write an original message using the special code. Each student then communicates with a student in a different class using the key, and the second student's job is to translate the code. Students can even swap classrooms using this technique and translate the code left in another student's desk. Make codes for younger students much simpler than for older ones.

WHEN: During a lesson

CONTENT STANDARD(S):   Abilities necessary to do scientific inquiry (5–12); Systems, order, and organization (5–12); Evidence, models, and explanation (5–12)

- Put students in cooperative groups of four to six. Using only 20 interlocking building blocks per group, have each group create a "space probe." As the groups assemble their probe, have one student in the group write directions to re-create the probe. Using only the written directions and the same 20 blocks, have students in another group try to create a duplicate of the original.

WHEN:	During a lesson
CONTENT STANDARD(S):	Position and motion of objects (K–4), Motions and forces (5–12), Transfer of energy (5–8), Interactions of energy and matter (9–12), Abilities necessary to do scientific inquiry (K–12), Understanding about scientific inquiry (K–12)

- Have students work cooperatively in an activity called a *marble roll.* Put students in groups of four to six. Give each group a mail tube (the containers used to carry and ship maps, posters, and so forth). Cut the mail tubes lengthwise to create U-shaped troughs. Place a marble in each trough. Have students in each group work together to carry the marble in a continuous forward motion to a predetermined location. The first student, when finished, moves to the end of the line. If the marble stops or goes backward, the group must start over. Each team records and graphs their trials.

WHEN:	During a lesson
CONTENT STANDARD(S):	All (K–12)

- When students are placed in cooperative groups and asked to teach one another what you just taught, they may be tempted to talk about something else. Just make a deal with them called *my stuff, your stuff.* Tell them to discuss *your stuff* first so that when you call on them, they will be prepared with an answer. After all, you are calling on nonvolunteers as well as volunteers. Then once they are prepared, they may talk about *their stuff.* What you will find is that when you give students opportunities to talk about what they wish, they are more likely to discuss what you wish!

REFLECTION AND APPLICATION

How will I incorporate *reciprocal teaching* and *cooperative learning* into instruction to engage students' brains?

Which reciprocal teaching and cooperative learning activities am I already incorporating into my science curriculum?

What additional activities will I incorporate?

Role Plays, Drama, Pantomimes, and Charades

WHAT: DEFINING THE STRATEGY

When I am teaching adults about how their brains operate and we get to the function of the hippocampus, I use a role play that turns out to be one of the favorite activities of the audience. We visualize that the entire room represents an actual human brain. Two participants volunteer to come to the front of the room and join palms together and raise their arms just as though they are playing London Bridge Is Falling Down. They represent the hippocampus, the gateway to long-term memory. Then, half of the class gets up and scatters to different places around the room while the remainder of the class observes the role play. The standing participants represent the bits and pieces of information in short-term, or working, memory in the brain. They must attempt to get into long-term memory or, in other words, to make their way through the hippocampus or gate. In order to get through the gate one at a time, they must be able to say their telephone number backward. Each participant writes their number on a piece of paper in advance so that the judge can verify the accuracy of the number as they pass through the hippocampus.

Then, the *information participants* line up and the parade begins. You should see grown men and women laughing uncontrollably while simultaneously rehearsing their backward phone numbers over and over again while they wait in line to get to a better place. If they make it in, they go and stand in an area of the room titled *long-term memory*. If they do not make it in, then they are rejected and go immediately to the *forgotten* area of the room.

Once the activity is completed, a whole-class discussion ensues during which participants determine what this role play has to do with the function of the hippocampus and which ways work best for getting information past it. Just imagine how many participants would ace the following request on a test after such a vivid role play: *Describe the function of the hippocampus.* Also, visualize how many of your students would ace your science test if you could find a way to incorporate role plays during instruction.

WHY: THEORETICAL FRAMEWORK

Dramatic plays or role plays foster interpersonal intelligence as described by Gardner. (Karten, 2007)

Teachers who use drama provide students with the lifelong gift of discovering their talents and feelings about expressing themselves while attempting to recall content. (Allen, 2008a)

Role plays engage students' emotions and strengthen their problem-solving skills while involving elements of spatial, verbal, linguistic, and kinesthetic modalities. (Jensen, E., 2004)

When students are involved in dramatic enactments, they physically role-play the content; but they must be able to explain how the enactment represents the information from the experience. (Marzano, 2007)

Learning which is physical is more engaging, motivating, and likely to be extended. (Jensen, E., 2008)

Every student should be encouraged to find a niche within the realm of drama or role play whether performing onstage or backstage. (Allen, 2008a)

Students are provided with emotional connections to real life when they are involved in the brain-based instructional strategies of role play and simulations. (Karten, 2007)

Test scores for classes where students were involved in minidramas or vignettes were significantly higher than scores in three additional classes taught next door with traditional methods. (Allen, 2008a)

Students are capable of comprehending content in new ways when their bodies are involved in the comprehension of role plays or skits. (Sprenger, 2007)

Role plays enable students to comprehend at much deeper levels than lecture since they not only access emotion but also use visual, spatial, linguistic, and bodily modalities. (Gregory & Parry, 2006)

Role plays are most effective when illustrating key events and showing the process of concepts that come in sequential order. (Udvari-Solner & Kluth, 2008)

Humor, as well as the arts, is so culturally pervasive because it assists us in distinguishing between appropriate and inappropriate behavior in make-believe rather than in real-life situations. (Sylwester, 2003)

HOW: INSTRUCTIONAL ACTIVITIES

WHEN: During a lesson

CONTENT STANDARD(S):   Position and motion of objects (K–4); Transfer of energy (5–8); Motions and forces (5–12); Interactions of energy and matter (9–12); Evidence, models, and explanations (K–12); Change, constancy, and measurement (K–12)

- Have students simulate atomic behavior that represents how sounds travel as atoms. Have 5 to 10 students line up, standing close together. Give the first student in the line a nudge forward. The other students will feel the energy go through them much like dominoes. This role play represents a solid where the atoms are close together. Now have the students stand farther apart to simulate a liquid and even farther apart to simulate a gas. Give the first student a nudge and examine the differences. Help them understand that sound travels much better through a solid than a gas. A rebound from the last person back to the first represents an echo.

WHEN: During a lesson

CONTENT STANDARD(S):   Changes in environments (K–4); Organisms and environments (K–4); Populations, resources, and environments (5–8); Nature of science (5–8); Diversity and adaptations of organisms (5–8); Biological evolution (9–12); Nature of scientific knowledge (9–12)

- Simulate various bird foods by placing beads, toothpicks, sunflower seeds, and so forth in the middle of the room on the floor. Include scraps of colored paper, some that would match the color of the floor. Place students in teams and have them compete for food by picking it up and bringing it back to the nest within a specified time. Some teams are given chopsticks for beaks, others have spoons, and still others have tweezers. Following the activity, have students analyze the types of foods that each team gathered. In addition, discuss how much of the food that blended into the floor color was gathered compared to the foods that were of brighter colors. This role play should lead to a discussion of adaptation and natural selection.

| **WHEN:** | During a lesson |
| **CONTENT STANDARD(S):** | Historical perspectives (9–12), Nature of scientific knowledge (9–12), Abilities necessary to do scientific inquiry (5–12), Understanding about scientific inquiry (5–12), Science as a human endeavor (5–12), Abilities of technological design (5–12), Understanding about science and technology (5–12) |

- Create a crime scene in your classroom with various clues, simulated blood, and other forms of evidence scattered throughout the room. Have students examine the evidence, use luminol to determine DNA, and piece together clues to write a hypothesis of what may have happened during the commission of the crime.

| **WHEN:** | During a lesson |
| **CONTENT STANDARD(S):** | Objects in the sky (K–4), Changes in earth and sky (K–4), Earth in the solar system (5–8), Origin and evolution of the universe (9–12) |

- Have students demonstrate an understanding of the rotation and revolution of the planets by dividing the class into groups of nine. One student in each group pretends to be the sun and the other eight pretend to be planets revolving around the sun in order from closest to the sun to farthest from the sun while simultaneously rotating on their axes. Give students signs to hold up for the planets that they represent so that other students have a visual.

| **WHEN:** | During a lesson |
| **CONTENT STANDARD(S):** | Position and motion of objects (K–4); Transfer of energy (5–8); Motions and forces (5–12); Interactions of energy and matter (9–12); Evidence, models, and explanation (K–12); Change, constancy, and measurement (K–12) |

- To teach the concept of pressure on atoms, have all students move to the center of the classroom. Place the desks around them in a circle. Have students move around slowly with their arms folded in front of them. If one student should bump into another student, they should bounce off and change direction while always moving in a straight line. Now with more energy, or a higher temperature, students should be bumping into the desks and pushing them outward. This role play should help students realize that pressure increases with temperature.

WHEN: During a lesson

CONTENT STANDARD(S): All (5–12)

- Turn one of your science units into a boot-camp unit, using ranks from the army, navy, marines, or coast guard. If there are multiple science classes in a school, each class could use a different branch of the military. Have students learn various science facts and concepts, which would enable them to receive a ranking. Learning more facts or receiving extra credit would help students reach the next rank. Students should strive to get the highest ranks possible. Have a graduation ceremony at the end of boot camp. When Warren Phillips actually conducted this activity with his science class, actual recruiting officers from various branches of the service donated posters, key fobs, and pens to use as prizes.

WHEN: During a lesson

CONTENT STANDARD(S): Organisms and environments (K–4), Populations and ecosystems (5–8), Interdependence of organisms (9–12)

- Using string, have students make a food web. Have each student role-play as though the individual is an organism in the environment. Then, ask each student to connect a string to any other student on which they are dependent. Students take turns making one connection of their choice. The person who receives the string makes the next connection. At some point during the role play, cut the string to show what extinction or pollution might do to upset a food web.

WHEN: During a lesson

CONTENT STANDARD(S): All (K–12)

- Review science vocabulary by playing charades. Write the words to be reviewed on separate 3" × 5" index cards. Divide the class into two heterogenous teams. Have one student from each team take turns coming to the front of the room, selecting a card at random, and acting out or role-playing the definition of the selected word. The student cannot speak but must use only gestures to get teammates to name the word. The team to guess the vocabulary word in the shortest amount of time wins a point for the team. The team with the most points at the culmination of the game is the winner. (Tate, 2010)

WHEN: During a lesson

CONTENT STANDARD(S): Properties of objects and materials (K–4), Properties and changes of properties in matter (5–8), Structure and properties of matter (9–12)

- Following a discussion of the properties of states of matter, have students pretend to be molecules. Divide the class into three groups. Have one group role-play as though they are solids by standing rigidly packed together; another group pretends to be liquids by moving around one another but not apart; and a third group role-plays molecules in gases by moving almost independently of one another and far apart. Those students in your class who exhibit characteristics of ADHD (attention-deficit-hyperactivity disorder) should be placed in the third group so that they can bounce around the room for a few seconds.

WHEN:	During a lesson
CONTENT STANDARD(S):	Science as a human endeavor (K–12); Evidence, models, and explanation (K–12); Abilities necessary to do scientific inquiry (K–12); Understanding about scientific inquiry (K–12)

- Locate a variety of field-trip sources that enable students to role-play science concepts. Check out the educational programs offered by local universities, laboratories, or nearby science museums. Some schools may even have access to facilities such as the McAuliffe Center, which enables students to participate in space simulations; Tomb, which offers an adventure using the scientific method; and City Lab, where students can simulate CSI investigations.

WHEN:	During a lesson
CONTENT STANDARD(S):	Populations, resources, and environments (5–8); Natural hazards (5–8); Risks and benefits (5–8); Natural resources (9–12); Environmental quality (9–12); Natural and human-induced hazards (9–12); Science and technology in local, national, and global challenges (9–12)

- Have students role-play as advocates for various forms of energy. Divide the class into solar, oil, coal, natural gas, and nuclear lobbyists. Have them research each energy form completely. Have them compete for funds from the Federal Reserve (represented by a small group of parents or other volunteers). One billion dollars is available, and they can ask for any percentage of the total. Have them make a presentation to you and the Federal Reserve. You will grade the presentations using a rubric developed by the class. Extra credit will be earned for any funds obtained from the Federal Reserve.

REFLECTION AND APPLICATION

How will I incorporate *role plays, drama, pantomimes,* and *charades* into instruction to engage students' brains?

Which role plays, drama, pantomimes, and charades am I already incorporating into my science curriculum?

What additional activities will I incorporate?

Strategy 15

Storytelling

WHAT: DEFINING THE STRATEGY

Allow me to tell you the following story:

Once upon a time, King Hiero II of Syracuse asked scientists to determine whether his crown was really made of gold or of some other material. The scientist, Archimedes, used reasoning, comparing the volume and weight of gold with the volume and weight of silver, which was the suspected substitute material in the king's crown. The only problem was that Archimedes did not know how to find the volume of an irregular object. One night, while he was taking a bath, he realized that if he would fill the bathtub completely with water and then catch all of the water that spilled over the edge once he got in that he would be able to tell the volume of his body. He was so excited by this discovery that he ran out into the streets naked, yelling, *Eureka!* (I've found it!) When Archimedes put the king's crown into the water, it displaced more water than the volume of gold, meaning that the goldsmith mixed silver with the gold when making the crown. The mystery had been solved!

This story can be used to help students remember Archimedes's contribution to the scientific community and to stimulate their thinking about all of the ways scientists solve problems. Since stories are connected together with a beginning, a middle, and an end, and the brain thinks in connections, storytelling is a natural strategy for facilitating memory. Stories are also nonthreatening and create an interest level that cannot be obtained in other ways. If you don't believe that is true, watch the next speaker or lecturer of a conference or workshop that you attend begin to tell a story. Notice that people in the audience pay rapt attention, and if the story is also funny or emotional, the attention and recall value is doubled. In addition, notice that you are still able, as an adult, to retell stories told to you as a child, all because of the power of this strategy.

WHY: THEORETICAL FRAMEWORK

Since even very young children acquire a sense of narrative, human beings naturally relate to stories. (Caine, Caine, McClintic, & Klimek, 2009)

Human beings have the uncanny ability to remember information embedded in stories, and it is the primary way humans passed down information for millennia. (Jensen, R., 2008)

The brain does not recall simple facts or concepts as well as it does stories. (Sprenger, 2007)

Semantic memory is activated by the contrasts, associations, and similarities that stories provide. (Markowitz & Jensen, 2007)

Storytelling can give students an opportunity to relate their feelings and personal meaning regarding content. (Jensen, R., 2008)

Curriculum can be connected to a larger purpose through storytelling and the activities that follow the story. (Caine, Caine, McClintic, & Klimek, 2009)

Information in our memory can be anchored by the script or schemata of a story. (Markowitz & Jensen, 2007)

Original stories, those created by the students, are often better remembered than the ones told by the teacher. (Allen, 2008a)

The brain thinks better in stories. (Damasio, 1999)

Storytelling ties information together and assists natural memory and, therefore, is a natural process for organizing information in the brain. (Caine & Caine, 1994)

Concrete images in stories activate our emotions and sense of meaning and supply cues and contexts for new information. (Markowitz & Jensen, 2007)

It may be easier for students to work in groups of three as they begin to create make-believe stories that include facts and people to be remembered. (Caine, Caine, McClintic & Klimek, 2005)

Information is bound in our memories to the scripts that stories can provide. (Markowitz & Jensen, 1999)

The sense of story that little children naturally develop and the brain fascination with it continue throughout their entire lives. (Caine, Caine, McClintic & Klimek, 2005)

HOW: INSTRUCTIONAL ACTIVITIES

WHEN: During a lesson

CONTENT STANDARD(S): All (K–12)

- Imitate Warren Phillips and in your classroom have a story bench or story stool where you sit in a nonthreatening environment and tell students stories related to a concept you are teaching. No notes are taken during a story so that students can give the story their undivided attention. If there are any important facts to be remembered, they are emphasized *after* the story for students to write down.

WHEN:	During a lesson
CONTENT STANDARD(S):	Abilities necessary to do scientific inquiry (K–12); Understanding about scientific inquiry (K–12); Systems, order, and organization (K–12); Evidence, models, and explanation (K–12)

- *Glyphs* are symbols that stand for various identifying characteristics. The late Dr. Carl Sagan (an American astrophysicist and author) helped NASA to design a set of glyphs about humans and the earth, which they sent into space to communicate with any life form that may find it. Have students interview one another and then tell a story of the other student's life using glyphs. For example, students can start with a face. A round face stands for a girl and an oval face for a boy. Each freckle on the face represents a sibling (* for boys and # for girls). Favorite foods are represented by eye shape. Pets are represented by nose shape. A necklace with varying symbols represents favorite activities of the student. The student draws a glyph of the information learned about the student they interviewed and then presents it to the class. See this book's companion website at www.corwin.com/scienceworksheets for a full lesson plan and handouts for a glyph activity.

WHEN:	During a lesson
CONTENT STANDARD(S):	History of science (5–8), Nature of scientific knowledge (9–12), Historical perspectives (9–12), Abilities necessary to do scientific inquiry (5–12), Understanding about scientific inquiry (5–12), Science as a human endeavor (5–12)

- There are many stories about scientists who have gone against social and religious mores. Have students read about these scientists and then retell the stories of their lives in writing. Great stories come from the following scientists' lives: Einstein, Galileo, Copernicus, Mendel, and Darwin.

WHEN:	During a lesson
CONTENT STANDARD(S):	History of science (5–8), Nature of scientific knowledge (9–12), Historical perspectives (9–12), Abilities necessary to do scientific inquiry (K–12), Science as a human endeavor (K–12), Understanding about scientific inquiry (K–12)

- Capture students' interests with the following stories about incidents of extreme pollution. They can then select one incident to research and write a story about as though they were reporting for a news broadcast.

- o **The Donora Smog Incident:** During this time of extreme smog from a steel plant in Pennsylvania, more than 20 people died in three days and hundreds of others were damaged for life.

- o **The Exxon *Valdez* Alaska Oil Spill:** During this environmental disaster, 10.8 million gallons of oil spilled and spread over 11,000 square miles.

- o **The Chernobyl Nuclear Accident:** Nuclear energy escaped in the Ukraine and killed 31 people immediately; however, radiation spread over 200,000 square miles and eventually, after 10 years, claimed the lives of 32,000. The accident also destroyed food harvests.

- o **The Cuyahoga River Fires:** Fires plagued the Cuyahoga River in Ohio beginning in 1936 when a spark from a blowtorch ignited floating debris and oil. The largest fire on the river in 1952 caused over $1 million in damage to boats and a riverfront office building. Fires erupted on the river several more times before June 22, 1969, when one of them captured the attention of *Time* magazine, which described the Cuyahoga as the river that "'oozes rather than flows' and in which a person 'does not drown but decays'" (Time Magazine, 1969).

- o **The BP Gulf of Mexico Oil Spill:** In 2010, the BP Gulf oil spill is unfolding as this book is written.

WHEN:	During a lesson
CONTENT STANDARD(S):	Diversity and adaptations of organisms (5–8); Biological evolution (9–12); Evolution and equilibrium (K–12); Understanding about scientific inquiry (K–12); Evidence, models, and explanation (K–12)

- Tell students the story of the *peppered moth* to help them understand the concept of natural selection. The story is as follows:

  The light-colored form of the moth was the predominant form in England prior to the beginning of the industrial revolution. Then darker-colored forms of the moth became much more prevalent. In areas where pollution had darkened the landscape, the darker moths were better camouflaged and less likely to be eaten by birds. Later, after the use of coal declined, under less-polluted conditions, the light-colored moths prevailed again. Go figure!

WHEN:	During a lesson
CONTENT STANDARD(S):	Organisms and environments (K–4), Structure and function in living systems (5–8), Behavior of organisms (9–12)

- As you study the digestive system, have students write a narrative story from a piece of food's point of view as it travels through the digestive tract. Have students weave in the necessary organs and relate the specific actions that take place at each organ from the food's perspective. The story should be written from a first person point of view.

WHEN: During a lesson

CONTENT STANDARD(S):   Properties and changes of properties in matter (5–8); Structure and properties of matter (9–12); Understanding about scientific inquiry (K–12); Evidence, models, and explanation (K–12)

- During a demonstration of pH and indicators, mesmerize the class by changing a clear liquid to purple, then back to clear, and then to milky white. Phenolphthalein is the indicator used. It turns colorless in acidic solutions and purple in basic solutions. It is milky white as a concentrate. Accompany the demonstration with the following story:

> My family is eating dinner and water is placed on the table for everyone to drink (place four glasses of clear liquid on a table). My son decides he wants a flavored drink mix (change one liquid to purple), but my daughter wants water. Then, my son changes his mind and decides he wants water also (change the liquid back to clear). Then, my spouse wants wine (change another clear liquid to purple), but I want a glass of milk (change another clear liquid to milky white).

In this demonstration the acidity and alkalinity of the liquid is varied and the indicator causes the color change. The key here is to develop a story around your science demonstrations. The demonstration and story can be used in conjunction with Warren Phillips's "The pH Song" (available for purchase online from iTunes) found on his CD *Sing-A-Long Science, The Second Sequel*.

WHEN: During a lesson

CONTENT STANDARD(S):   Properties of objects and materials (K–4); Properties and changes of properties in matter (5–8); Motions and forces (5–12); Interactions of energy and matter (9–12); Evidence, models, and explanation (K–12)

- Tell students the following story of amber to help them understand the discovery of electricity:

Amber is a rock made from the sap of prehistoric trees. Sometimes, insects became trapped in this sap. In ancient times, people noticed that the sap had magical powers. Specifically, it attracted straw and certain other materials when it was rubbed. This magical power is called *static electricity*. Since the Latin word for amber is *electrum*, this force became known as electricity and later the particles of attraction in the atom were called *electrons*. We now know that these particles can escape from atoms and are called free radicals or free electrons. These free radicals can accumulate as static electricity. If enough of them accumulate in the air, they create lightning!

WHEN: During a lesson

CONTENT STANDARD(S):   All (K–8)

- There are authors of children's books who specialize in science content. One such author is Jerry Pallota, who writes a series of science alphabet books. Some of his book titles include the following: *The Ocean Alphabet Book* (1989), *The Dinosaur Alphabet Book* (1990a), and *The Frog Alphabet Book* (1990b).

WHEN: After a lesson

CONTENT STANDARD(S):   History of science (5–8), Nature of scientific knowledge (9–12), Historical perspectives (9–12), Abilities necessary to do scientific inquiry (K–12), Understanding about scientific inquiry (K–12), Science as a human endeavor (K–12)

- There have been many scientific discoveries that were accidental. Have students make a class book of stories where each student chooses and researches one accidental discovery. A good source with dozens of examples is the *People's Almanac* (a series of three books by David Wallechinsky and Irving Wallace, published in 1975, 1978, and 1981). Many fascinating favorites include the following: chocolate chip cookies, cola, Popsicles, aspartame sweetener, brandy, Teflon, the microwave, potato chips, penicillin, and sticky notes.

WHEN: After a lesson

CONTENT STANDARD(S):   All (5–12)

- Have students create stories, fictional or fact, that can be used to remember a concept that has been taught. Stories are particularly helpful when recalling a multistep process or events that happen in sequential order. Have students retell their stories several times to their classmates. Have them recall their original stories each time they attempt to remember the key concept.

REFLECTION AND APPLICATION

> How will I incorporate *storytelling* into instruction to engage students' brains?

Which storytelling activities am I already incorporating into my science curriculum?

What additional activities will I incorporate?

Strategy 16

Technology

WHAT: DEFINING THE STRATEGY

A biology teacher goes to sleep at night and dreams of the following class-room: Students are working in cooperative groups or families and seated at lab tables so that conversation is easily facilitated. At the front of the room is an interactive whiteboard with a document camera attached. In the dream, the teacher is using the document camera to display an experiment for a small group of students so that they can replicate it the next day for the remainder of the class. Three students are in the back of the room on the Internet doing research for a report on the types of animals found in a rain-forest. Four other students are using a video projector that is attached to one microscope. This will enable them to more plainly see the process of mitosis as cells divide. Several students have brought water in from a creek near their homes so that they can look for the presence of paramecium. Every student is actively engaged in some way in this technologically savvy class-room where learning is facilitated and students feel at home with the tech-nology. The teacher then awakens and discovers that the dream is not a fantasy. It is actually a reality in many classrooms around the world.

In a recent issue of *USA Today*, the writer talks of a new generation of students, younger than the Millennial generation, who have so grown up with technology that they know of nothing else. These students are sitting in elementary and middle schools right now and are so conversant with computers, text messages, voice mails, and the Internet that they are teach-ing their parents and teachers a thing or two. After all, it was my 25-year-old daughter who gave me staff development lessons on the use of the iPod, as opposed to a CD player, for the music in my workshops. Now that I am in the habit of using an iPod, I cannot imagine using anything else.

Please remember, however, that technology is only one of 20 strategies that take advantage of the way brains learn best. You should not neglect the other 19 if you wish to produce highly literate, well-rounded, socially capable, mentally and physically healthy human beings.

WHY: THEORETICAL FRAMEWORK

The Internet is increasingly used as a tool for learning science. (National Research Council of the National Academies, 2006)

Students of today should be *technologically literate* with a working knowledge of the following: keyboarding, using databases, reading technical manuals, using wireless technology, Web-based learning, and programs for multimedia presentations. (Fogarty, 2009, p. 95)

Activities that encourage students to use both inductive and deductive reasoning as well as those that involve the use of computers or computational skills engage students' logical-mathematical intelligence. (Karten, 2007)

Students who do not have the appropriate technological tools when they graduate are not equipped to do postsecondary study or enter the world of work. (Fogarty, 2009)

Technology is not the lesson itself but only a tool for delivering the lesson. (Hiraoka, 2006)

Over the last 20 years, personal computers have enabled people to develop software for the express purpose of helping students learn science. (National Research Council of the National Academies, 2006)

Computer software can help teachers show students conceptual relationships between theory and natural phenomena or help them explore and observe simulations that would be too dangerous or expensive to be experienced in real life. (National Research Council of the National Academies, 2006)

The most successful science instructional sequences have students work in small groups to integrate computer simulations with real laboratory experiences. (Bell, 2005)

Students of all ability levels can use technology to "process, demonstrate, retain, and share information and communication." (Karten, 2009, p. 196)

Literacy in the digital age refers not only to writing and reading but also to a student's ability to use technology when analyzing the volume of information that exists. (Sheffield, 2007)

A number of students who are failing traditional classroom courses are able to avail themselves of technology-based courses in an effort to catch up with their peers. (Barr & Parrett, 2007)

Interactive technology (such as computer animation programs or HyperStudio) makes learning fun and exciting for adolescents. (Feinstein, 2009)

HOW: INSTRUCTIONAL ACTIVITIES

WHEN: During a lesson

CONTENT STANDARD(S): Abilities of technological design (K–12), Understanding about science and technology (K–12), Understanding about scientific inquiry (K–12), Abilities necessary to do scientific inquiry (K–12)

- Involve students in content with the use of an interactive whiteboard (such as a SMART or Promethean board). These technological presentation devices enable the teacher to access the Internet and display it to the entire class as well as show the class other computer programs of interest. Some boards can also be used to display regular writing when done with the special markers provided.

WHEN: During or after a lesson

CONTENT STANDARD(S): Abilities of technological design (K–12), Understanding about science and technology (K–12), Understanding about scientific inquiry (K–12), Abilities necessary to do scientific inquiry (K–12)

- Have students view an online video about a topic recently discussed in science class. Information can be downloaded and viewed as a computer slide-show presentation. (Discovery Science's United Streaming at www.streaming.discoveryeducation.com provides a multimedia library of educational videos and images. Another online video source could be YouTube at www.youtube.com or Teacher Tube at www.teachertube.com.)

WHEN: During a lesson

CONTENT STANDARD(S): Characteristics of organisms (K–4); Structure and function in living systems (5–8); Understanding about science and technology (K–12); Systems, order, and organization (K–12); Matter, energy, and organization in living systems (9–12)

- Have students play the game Scramble. They must have a notebook and pen or pencil to play. Scramble the letters of an animal or plant, and give the letters orally one at a time to pairs of students. Students are able to ask for one-letter clues until one student is the first to unscramble the word. Then, designated students sitting at computers rush to be the first to find the plant or animal on the Internet. They must find a picture and scientific name on the same website in order to win. The two students with the most wins get to sit in a soft *cushy* chair for the day.

WHEN: During a lesson

CONTENT STANDARD(S):   Characteristics of organisms (K–4), Structure and function in living systems (5–8), Behavior of organisms (9–12), Abilities necessary to do scientific inquiry (K–12), Understanding about scientific inquiry (K–12)

- Have students use calculators to expedite their ability to solve scientific problems such as the following: If rabbits have 10 babies per litter and reproduce every six months, how many rabbits will there be after two years? Three years? Four years?

WHEN: During a lesson

CONTENT STANDARD(S):   Abilities of technological design (K–12), Understanding about science and technology (K–12), Understanding about scientific inquiry (K–12), Abilities necessary to do scientific inquiry (K–12)

- Peruse the following outstanding websites to be used with your science students:
  - Explore Learning: www.explorelearning.com (free trial) provides simulations of labs and interactive experiments.
  - Brainpop: www.brainpop.com (free trial) provides short cartoon videos that teach science concepts.
  - NASA: www.nasa.gov provides many great videos, pictures, and labs.
  - Google Earth: http://earth.google.com provides great maps and information on any site in the world and also contains a tour of the solar system and the universe.
  - E-Pals Global Community: www.epals.com connects over 11 million students and teachers from 191 countries building skills and enhancing learning.
  - Wikispaces: www.wikispaces.com is a free website where students can create individual webpages or can form a community for online discussions.
  - PBS: www.pbs.org/wgbh/aso/tryit provides interactive try-it labs.
  - Exploratorium: www.exploratorium.edu is an interactive website that has ongoing exploration of science, art, and human perception.

WHEN: During a lesson

CONTENT STANDARD(S):   Characteristics of organisms (K–4), Structure and function in living systems (5–8), Behavior of organisms (9–12), Abilities necessary to do scientific inquiry (K–12), Understanding about scientific inquiry (K–12)

- Using a calculator, have students measure their response to a stimulus. Drop a meter stick between the thumb and palm of a student's open hand. As the student grabs the meter stick, have another student measure the distance in centimeters that the ruler dropped. Have all students graph the results on a computer spreadsheet program.

WHEN:	During a lesson
CONTENT STANDARD(S):	Characteristics of organisms (K–4), Structure and function in living systems (5–8), Behavior of organisms (9–12), Abilities necessary to do scientific inquiry (K–12), Understanding about scientific inquiry (K–12)

- Probes and sensors are excellent tools to help students visualize results as they occur. There are many types of probes and sensors and most are linked to excellent graphing software. The site www.vernier.com/probes is recommended for a great variety of experiments.

WHEN:	During a lesson
CONTENT STANDARD(S):	Abilities of technological design (K–12), Understanding about science and technology (K–12), Understanding about scientific inquiry (K–12), Abilities necessary to do scientific inquiry (K–12)

- Integrate science curriculum with technology: Combine interactive science toys with technology. Online science education companies (such as CPO Science—Cambridge Physics Outlet—at www.cpo.com) feature completely integrated materials. Systems can include a student text, investigations manual, equipment, teacher's guide, and resource material with technology tools for planning and enhancing student learning.

WHEN:	During or after a lesson
CONTENT STANDARD(S):	Abilities of technological design (K–12), Understanding about science and technology (K–12), Understanding about scientific inquiry (K–12), Abilities necessary to do scientific inquiry (K–12)

- Have students use collaborative webpages (such as www.wiki-spaces.com or www.wikispaces.com/site/for/teachers), which classes can edit together, to discuss a recent event in science class or to voice an opinion online that can be read by classmates. Online pages provide a place to have group discussions that only your students, or the entire world, can view. Different classes can work collaboratively on the same project. You can restrict who participates, ensuring that no outsiders interfere with your students' ideas.

WHEN:	During or after a lesson
CONTENT STANDARD(S):	Understanding about scientific inquiry (K–12), Science as a human endeavor (K–12), Abilities of technological design (K–12), Understanding about science and technology (K–12)

- Have students create a time line of technological advances over the last 100 years. This time line could encompass just the past 20 years or could even cover a period within the students' lifetime. Each student can work on one invention and the class can cooperatively assemble the time line.

WHEN:	During or after a lesson
CONTENT STANDARD(S):	Abilities necessary to do scientific inquiry (K–12), Abilities of technological design (K–12), Understanding about science and technology (K–12)

- Have students create videos of their oral presentations of their science projects in addition to backboards, posters, or written reports. A free program called Photo Story 3 (Microsoft, 2005) can be downloaded from the Microsoft website for this purpose. Students can combine pictures, transitions, audio recordings, and music to create a powerful presentation.

Warren Phillips's Website

Many links and lots of science information, as well as details on how to do a science fair project, are available at www.wphillips.com.

REFLECTION AND APPLICATION

> How will I incorporate *technology* into instruction
> to engage students' brains?

Which technological activities am I already incorporating into my science curriculum?

What additional activities will I incorporate?

Strategy 17

Visualization and Guided Imagery

WHAT: DEFINING THE STRATEGY

Mrs. Patrick, a chemistry teacher, related this story to me. Every day as she reviewed the elements on the periodic table, she would stand on the lab table and point to each element as students named them out loud. While students' heads bobbed up and down to the rhythm of the pointer, the elements were remembered. On test day, Mrs. Patrick took the chart off the wall so that it would not serve as a ready reference. She wanted to know whether the students could recall the elements from memory. What she didn't know was that it didn't matter whether the chart was on the wall or not. As students were taking the test, they were staring at the wall visualizing the chart and Mrs. Patrick pointing to the elements as they were named. She even witnessed students' heads bobbing up and down as they were answering the questions on the test.

According to the brain research, when one visualizes, the brain goes through the same processes it would if it were actually experiencing the event. That is why athletes visualize themselves scoring the touchdown or hitting the homerun before the game even begins. Visualization improves the quality of the athlete's performance, and it can improve the quality of the work of your students as well. On the first day of school, have students visualize themselves making A's in your class as they participate in some of the same real-world activities that a scientist would.

WHY: THEORETICAL FRAMEWORK

"If a picture is worth a thousand words, perhaps drawing and visualization can help science students enhance their learning potential." (National Science Teachers Association [NSTA], 2006, p. 20)

Rehearsing events in your mind helps you locate pertinent information and preexposes you to important data. (Jensen, E., 2008)

"A picture in your mind creates a memory you can find." (Sprenger, 2007, p. 33)

Imagery gives us more mind-body control and changes body chemistry. (Markowitz & Jensen, 2007)

When students are visualizing, the very same parts of the brain's visual cortex are activated as when the eyes are actually taking in and processing information from the real world. (Sousa, 2006)

A vivid imagination that is fun, absurd, surreal, or humorous creates images that have staying power. (Markowitz & Jensen, 2007)

Teachers can ask students to visualize or vividly imagine what is going on during a chemical process while the student is reading about it. (Caine, Caine, McClintic, & Klimek, 2005)

Coaches know that athletes perform better when they mentally rehearse their performance than when they do not use imagery. (Sousa, 2006)

Visualization, or making mental pictures of sensory images, is one of eight thinking strategies effective readers use to comprehend text. (Daniels & Zemelman, 2004)

A meta-analysis of 1,500 students representing nine separate studies showed that those who visualized or used more mental imagery while learning engaged in creativity during discussions, modeling, and assessments. (LeBoutillier & Marks, 2003)

When competent and struggling eighth-grade readers were compared, competent readers appear to visualize what they are reading while those who are struggling do not. (Wilhelm, 1997)

When nothing else worked, role plays, particularly prior to reading, were quite effective in helping students visualize what they were reading. They helped students picture the action in their heads. (Wilhelm, 1997)

If the majority of classroom time was spent ensuring that students are forming proper images, the instructor's work would be infinitely facilitated. The image is the greatest instrument of instruction. (Dewey, 1938)

HOW: INSTRUCTIONAL ACTIVITIES

WHEN: Before a lesson

CONTENT STANDARD(S):   All (K–12)

- Have students use predictive visualization to imagine what something might look, sound, or feel like before beginning the lesson. This technique helps them to use their background knowledge and to make a connection to the topic.

WHEN: Before a lesson

CONTENT STANDARD(S):   All (K–12)

- To alleviate anxiety prior to any science test, have students take deep breaths and visualize themselves successfully completing each item on the test. This activity, in addition to well-taught lessons incorporating the brain-compatible strategies, gives students the confidence they need to do well! (Tate, 2010)

WHEN: Before a lesson

CONTENT STANDARD(S):   All (5–12)

- Have students read through the sequence of steps in a lab they are getting ready to complete. Then, have them visualize each step. You may want them to provide an illustration for several of the steps to facilitate their understanding of the laboratory procedures. (Ogle, 2000)

WHEN: During a lesson

CONTENT STANDARD(S):   Changes in earth and sky (K–4), Structure of the earth system (5–8), Energy in the earth system (9–12), Geochemical cycles (9–12), Evolution and equilibrium (K–12)

- Have students visualize and describe the sights, sounds, temperatures, and smells of a lava flow from an erupting volcano. Go Visit Hawaii at www.govisithawaii.com has blogs where visitors have described their sensations at the site of a lava flow.

WHEN: During a lesson

CONTENT STANDARD(S):   Evidence, models, and explanation (K–12); Change, constancy, and measurement (K–12); Evolution and equilibrium (K–12)

- Have students read or read aloud to them a book like *The Giving Tree* (Silverstein, 1964) to help them visualize the effects of people on the ecosystem.

WHEN: During a lesson

CONTENT STANDARD(S):   Regulation and behavior (5–8); Matter, energy, and organization in living systems (9–12); Form and function (K–12)

- Have students visualize and describe the molecules of food as they are absorbed into the cell, stored in the vacuoles, broken down by the lysosomes, brought to the mitochondria, and broken into energy (ATP, adenosine triphosphate) and, finally, as they leave the cell as CO_2 (carbon dioxide) and H_2O (water).

WHEN: During a lesson

CONTENT STANDARD(S):   All (5–12)

- Have students work individually or in groups to create visual images that link a word to its definition. The more absurd the visual image, the easier it is for the brain to remember the definition. For example, to remember the definition of *hippocampus,* a part of the brain that determines what information will eventually get into long-term memory, have students visualize a herd of hippopotamus walking on a college campus through a gate. This image depicts the hippocampus as the *gateway to long-term memory.* (Tate, 2010)

WHEN: During a lesson

CONTENT STANDARD(S):   Position and motion of objects (K–4); Motions and forces (5–8); Structure and properties of matter (9–12); Evidence, models, and explanation (K–12)

- A *vacuum* is a space with no atoms. Most people think that things get sucked into a vacuum, but this is not the case. The atoms outside of a vacuum get pushed into the area with no atoms. To help students understand this concept, have students visualize a classroom with 200 students in it. The room next door has no students. Have them imagine that someone opens the door between the rooms and students begin to push other students into the empty room. Eventually, there will be equilibrium or an equal number of students in each room.

WHEN: During a lesson

CONTENT STANDARD(S):   Organisms and environments (K–4); Diversity and adaptations of organisms (5–8); Matter, energy, and organization in living systems (9–12); Systems, order, and organization (K–12); Evidence, models, and explanation (K–12)

- To help students understand how sound travels through air, have them visualize sound vibrating the eardrum, causing the hammer to hit the anvil and vibrating the cochlea with liquid inside. Have them picture the liquid sloshing back and forth moving the cilia hairs, which are attached to nerve cells that travel to the brain. Have them "see" the brain creating the sound from incoming information.

WHEN: During a lesson

CONTENT STANDARD(S):   Organisms and environments (K–4); Diversity and adaptations of organisms (5–8); Matter, energy, and organization in living systems (9–12); Systems, order, and organization (K–12); Evidence, models, and explanation (K–12)

- Have students visualize the white blood cells in the body changing shapes (since they are amoeboid), squeezing through the blood vessels to go to the site of an injury. Have them picture the white blood cells attacking foreign cells by surrounding and engulfing them. Some continue to attach to fibrinogen (a spiderweb-like protein that unravels) to stop blood flow at the site of a cut by creating a scab.

WHEN: During a lesson

CONTENT STANDARD(S):   Properties of earth materials (K–4); Earth's history (5–8); Geochemical cycles (9–12); Origin and evolution of the earth system (9–12); Evolution and equilibrium (K–12); Evidence, models, and explanation (K–12); Change, constancy, and measurement (K–12)

- Have students visualize a rock as it changes from sedimentary, to igneous, to metamorphic, and back to sedimentary. The visualization can be followed by an assignment during which students write the conditions and forces necessary for this process to occur.

WHEN: During a lesson

CONTENT STANDARD(S):   Position and motion of objects (K–4); Motions and forces (5–8); Structure and properties of matter (9–12); Evidence, models, and explanation (K–12)

- Have students visualize the following to help them understand things on an atomic scale. Have them visualize a large domed stadium like the Houston Astrodome. If they don't know what a dome looks like, show them a visual. Tell them that if a proton is the size of a ping-pong ball, the electron going around it would be located at the top of the Houston Astrodome. It is unbelievable, but empty space makes up 99.9% of an atom.

WHEN: After a lesson

CONTENT STANDARD(S):   Characteristics of organisms (K–4); Structure and function in living systems (5–8); Matter, energy, and organization in living systems (9–12); Systems, order, and organization (K–12)

- Following a lesson on the digestive system, have students visualize the trip of food through that system. This activity can be aided with Warren Phillips's "Digestion Song" found on his CD *Sing-A-Long Science*. The CD can be located on Warren's website at www.wphillips.com.

REFLECTION AND APPLICATION

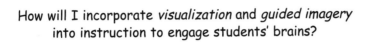

How will I incorporate *visualization* and *guided imagery*
into instruction to engage students' brains?

*Which visualization and guided imagery activities am I already
incorporating into my science curriculum?*

What additional activities will I incorporate?

Strategy 18

Visuals

WHAT: DEFINING THE STRATEGY

I read recently in a scientific periodical that the visual cortex in the brains of some students today is actually thicker than the visual cortex in the brains of people my age. This is due to the fact that so much of today's information comes into the brain visually. Students are watching large amounts of television, they are spending countless hours on the computer or playing video games, or they are reading numerous text messages. By the way, these sedentary activities are part of the reason that we are seeing Type 2 diabetes earlier than ever before. Both the brain and body need physical movement. The National Football League (NFL) has created a program called Play 60 encouraging students to engage in at least 60 minutes of active play per day. See Strategy 10: Movement in this book for ideas that help students become more active while learning. But, I digress!

The visual modality is a strong one for many students. Since a picture is worth a thousand words, science teachers would do well to capitalize on this strength. Perform a science demonstration for students to see prior to expecting them to replicate it, take a virtual field trip and have students watch an interactive lab online, have students create a video presentation to accompany their science fair project, or even change your location in the room as you teach so that you maintain your students' interest. Remember to *teach on your feet, not in your seat!* Place pertinent visuals on your walls in your science classroom. Even the peripheral vision of students matters. A model of the periodic table or the steps in the scientific process on the wall have strong effects on the brains of students as they take in the information gleaned from those visuals on a daily basis.

WHY: THEORETICAL FRAMEWORK

When students conceptualize, design, and polish their own visual creations, they remember them better than if someone else created them. (Allen, 2008a)

Assist your visual learners by (1) using words that are visually related such as *I see what you mean* or *Take a look at this;* (2) show slides, drawings, pictures, or words on the board; and (3) move around the classroom so that students remain in your field of vision. (Jensen, E., 2009)

Since most of the brain's learning is unconscious, posters, drawings, and other peripherals on the wall can powerfully influence the brain. (Jensen, E., 2004)

Since the educational system and society as a whole are dependent on visuals, it is crucial that teachers support students' visual modalities. (Sprenger, 2007)

Visual scientific representations include pictures, graphs, charts, physical models, or diagrams, which can convey a scientific idea but can also have limitations and convey incorrect ideas. (Keeley, 2008)

Visuals such as concept maps, graphic icons, sketches, flowcharts, and drawings assist students in understanding and processing new content. (Allen, 2008a)

A student's brain can "register more than 36,000 images per hour" and the eyes can take in 30 million pieces of information per second making visuals key to effective instruction. (Jensen, E., 2004, p. 18)

Thinking with visuals (murals, drawings, computer graphics, and paintings) is an effective tool for elaboration since words and pictures can show great detail. (Jensen, E., 2009)

Visual aids provide students with a point of focus and improve learning as students encounter the following stages of acquiring new concepts: "acquisition, proficiency, maintenance, and generalization." (Algozzine, Campbell, & Wang, 2009a, p. 72)

Pictures can interfere with a person's ability to listen to the words when the visuals and the auditory used to explain the visuals do not go together. (Posamentier & Jaye, 2006)

The effects of direct instruction on students' brains diminish after about two weeks, but when students are looking at visuals, even peripherally, those effects increase during the same two-week period. (Jensen, E., 2004)

Since visuals can be quickly remembered by the brain, they are often more powerful than words in communicating a teacher's message. (Allen, 2008a)

HOW: INSTRUCTIONAL ACTIVITIES

WHEN:	Before a lesson
CONTENT STANDARD(S):	Systems, order, and organization (K–12); Evidence, models, and explanation (K–12); Abilities necessary to do scientific inquiry (K–12); Understanding about scientific inquiry (K–12)

- Using wood putty, create models that can be used as visuals for your students year after year as you teach certain science concepts. Models that can be made include a cell, a volcano, a glacier, and the earth's layers. Paint the models and place them on a piece of plywood to save for later use.

WHEN:	Before a lesson
CONTENT STANDARD(S):	Systems, order, and organization (K–12); Evidence, models, and explanation (K–12); Abilities necessary to do scientific inquiry (K–12); Understanding about scientific inquiry (K–12)

- Place charts, graphs, or organizers on the walls to reinforce the science content to be studied. For example, the periodic table on the wall serves as a constant visual reminder of the elements.

WHEN:	Before or during a lesson
CONTENT STANDARD(S):	All (K–12)

- Start a collection of materials related to a unit of study, such as a rock collection as you begin a unit on rocks. For example, have rock samples and streak plates that students can use when studying the three types of rocks. A streak plate produces a fine powder when a mineral is rubbed against its hard surface. The color of the powder is used as an identifying characteristic. Warren has used a display case for this collection, changing its contents with each unit.

WHEN:	Before or during a lesson
CONTENT STANDARD(S):	All (5–12)

- If you add pictures and humor to your science study guide, those guides can make great visuals and students look forward to reading and studying them.

WHEN:	Before or after a lesson
CONTENT STANDARD(S):	Science as a human endeavor (K–12), Nature of scientific knowledge (9–12), Abilities necessary to do scientific inquiry (9–12), Understanding about scientific inquiry (9–12)

• Create a "wall of accomplishment" that shows off the great work that individual students or classes have done. The wall starts off as blank in September and accumulates exhibits as the year progresses.

WHEN:	During a lesson
CONTENT STANDARD(S):	Abilities necessary to do scientific inquiry (K–12), Understanding about scientific inquiry (K–12)

• As you deliver a lecturette, or minilecture, provide students with a visual by filling in a semantic map or creating an appropriate graphic organizer emphasizing the lecturette's main ideas and key points. Place the map or organizer on the board. Lecturettes typically last less than seven minutes. (See Strategy 5: Graphic Organizers, Semantic Maps, and Word Webs for specific examples.)

WHEN:	During a lesson
CONTENT STANDARD(S):	Characteristics of organisms (K–4); Structure and function in living systems (5–8); Systems, order, and organization (K–12)

• Using an apron in a solid, light color, draw a life-size picture of the digestive system or the skeletal system on the apron. Color and label the parts. As you wear the apron in class, it will serve as a visual reminder of the concept you are teaching. You can also buy plastic aprons with the visuals already imprinted on them.

WHEN:	During a lesson
CONTENT STANDARD(S):	Systems, order, and organization (K–12); Evidence, models, and explanation (K–12); Abilities necessary to do scientific inquiry (K–12); Understanding about scientific inquiry (K–12)

• Use an overhead or a document camera to show experiments and demonstrations to the entire class at one time. Many experiments can be shown very effectively in this way, and a valuable visual is provided.

WHEN:	During a lesson
CONTENT STANDARD(S):	Systems, order, and organization (K–12); Evidence, models, and explanation (K–12); Abilities necessary to do scientific inquiry (K–12); Understanding about scientific inquiry (K–12)

- Add a video projector to your microscope. This projector allows all students to see what specific processes look like such as an air bubble, focus techniques, or fantastic discoveries of an organism. Connect the video projector to a VCR or DVD recorder to create a permanent record of great discoveries by students.

WHEN: During a lesson

CONTENT STANDARD(S):   Systems, order, and organization (5–12); Evidence, models, and explanation (5–12); Abilities necessary to do scientific inquiry (5–12); Understanding about scientific inquiry (5–12)

- Get an atom kit and use it to construct molecules such as glucose, salt, water, carbon dioxide, and DNA. The molecule construction serves as a visual for the class to replicate.

WHEN: During a lesson

CONTENT STANDARD(S):   Systems, order, and organization (K–12); Evidence, models, and explanation (K–12); Abilities necessary to do scientific inquiry (K–12); Understanding about scientific inquiry (K–12)

- Introduce working models, such as motors, pumping hearts, or electricity kits, to serve as visuals for students during a lesson.

WHEN: During a lesson

CONTENT STANDARD(S):   Characteristics of organisms (K–4); Structure and function in living systems (5–8); Diversity and adaptations of organisms (5–8); Matter, energy, and organization in living systems (9–12); Form and function (K–12)

- Explain the process of photosynthesis by using 2-D models, circles with magnets on a magnetic board, for each kind of atom (6 carbon, 24 hydrogen, 24 oxygen). Visually demonstrate how these atoms form molecules.

$$12H_2O + 6CO_2 \rightarrow C_6H_{12}O_6 + 6H_2O + 6O_2$$

This visual is important in showing students that the same atoms are used and reorganized into glucose.

WHEN:	During a lesson
CONTENT STANDARD(S):	Systems, order, and organization (K–12); Evidence, models, and explanation (K–12); Abilities necessary to do scientific inquiry (K–12); Understanding about scientific inquiry (K–12)

- Have visuals that do not compete with your lesson. For example, if you present a computer slide show, students will want to take notes from it rather than listen to you, so provide a miniature copy of the slides for students to record notes on. Be sure your visuals and your voice go together.

WHEN:	During a lesson
CONTENT STANDARD(S):	Characteristics of organisms (K–4); Structure and function in living systems (5–8); Behavior of organisms (9–12); Abilities necessary to do scientific inquiry (K–12); Understanding about scientific inquiry (K–12)

- Like Warren Phillips, incorporate a fish tank into your classroom every year. Begin with an empty tank. Tell students that the tank belongs to them. Have them bring in gravel and decorations for the tank and, more important, the fish that the tank will contain. Have students name the fish and show them off to the class. Get them involved in tank maintenance. The sights and sounds of this tank are important relaxing components to a calming and productive classroom environment conducive to optimal learning.

REFLECTION AND APPLICATION

How will I incorporate *visuals* into instruction to engage students' brains?

Which visuals am I already incorporating into my science curriculum?

What additional visuals will I incorporate?

Work Study and Apprenticeships

WHAT: DEFINING THE STRATEGY

Many years ago in a workshop, a presenter told the story of an experiment conducted by Marian Diamond, a brain researcher at UCLA. Three groups of mice were placed in three different conditions. One group of mice was placed in cages all by themselves. They did not have any other mice to talk to; they had no wheels to run on, no toys to play with, and very little to engage their brains. After a period of time, the dendrites, or brain cells, that they grew were measured. As you might imagine, not many brain cells were grown. The second group of mice was placed in cages with other mice. I don't know exactly what mice talk about, but they were able to communicate. These mice had wheels to run on and lots of toys to engage their brains and bodies. Do you think they grew more or fewer dendrites than the first group? If you said more, you would be correct. The third group of mice was placed in a simulated real-world environment. They had to solve problems in the real world: how to find food, how to find shelter, and so forth. The growth in the number of brain cells was exponentially greater, leading us to believe that, at least in mice brains, dendrites grow better in the real world than in artificial environments.

While scientists caution us about drawing conclusions about the working of the human brain based on what happens in the laboratory with mice brains, the results do give us some food for thought. Could it be that school is artificial for the human brain? After all, it is about the only place in the real world where a person cannot talk or move for hours at a time.

Work study, apprenticeships, practicums, and internships may be instructional strategies that afford students the best of both worlds: exposure in school to a wide variety of real-world experiences that help students determine possible career choices and actual on-the-job work experiences that prepare students for success in the real world. For example, I was presenting for the Circle Unified School District in Towanda, Kansas. I was being driven to the high school when the driver showed me three houses in the neighborhood that had been built by students in the vocational program. The houses were beautifully constructed and already occupied. Imagine the real-world skills and abilities these students are acquiring as they participate in the high school's work-study program.

WHY: THEORETICAL FRAMEWORK

New learning becomes more relevant when students are taught to connect new learning with things within their real world. (Allen, 2008a)

It becomes problematic when high school students are covering a great deal of content without the opportunity to use the content within the context of authentic situations. (Wiggins & McTighe, 2008)

Students need opportunities to interact within the larger context of solving real-world problems and conflicting situations. (Caine, Caine, McClintic, & Klimek, 2005)

When teachers relate the skills they teach to the personal lives of their students, they are engaging in real-life teaching. (Breaux & Whitaker, 2006)

The schoolwork of adolescents must take them into the "dynamic life of their environments." (Brooks, 2002, p. 72)

Educated adults often have difficulty finding a job or meeting job expectations since large gaps can exist between the performance needed to be successful in a business setting and the performance required for school success. (Sternberg & Grigorenko, 2000)

The strongest neural networks are created when students are actually engaged in real-life experiences and not from tasks that are not authentic. (Westwater & Wolfe, 2000)

When students learn under the supervision of an expert in the field, they are given full participation in the process of learning and working. (Wonacott, 1993)

Learning should be organized around cognitive-apprenticeship principles, which stress subject-specific content and the skills required to function within the content. (Berryman & Bailey, 1992)

When students observe and confer with an expert, they build technical skills and share tasks that relate those technical skills to their knowledge and interpretation. (Wonacott, 1993)

HOW: INSTRUCTIONAL ACTIVITIES

WHEN: Before, during, or after a lesson

CONTENT STANDARD(S): Science and technology in local challenges (K–4); Science and technology in society (5–8); Nature of science (5–8); Science and technology in local, national, and global challenges (9–12); Science as a human endeavor (K–12); Nature of scientific knowledge (9–12)

- Initiate a career day in your school. Invite parents, dignitaries, local celebrities, radio station hosts, scientists, and persons of interest to talk about their vocations or avocations. This can be done school-wide or within your individual classroom.

WHEN: Before, during, or after a lesson

CONTENT STANDARD(S): Science and technology in local challenges (K–4); Science and technology in society (5–8); Nature of science (5–8); Science and technology in local, national, and global challenges (9–12); Science as a human endeavor (K–12); Nature of scientific knowledge (9–12)

- When you have a student who has had extreme difficulty with classroom behavior, have them shadow a professional—such as a teacher, a paraprofessional, a custodian, a school painter, or a groundskeeper—around the school doing their daily work. Have them become an assistant and allow them to continue shadowing if their classroom behavior is acceptable.

WHEN: During a lesson

CONTENT STANDARD(S): Science and technology in local challenges (K–4); Science and technology in society (5–8); Nature of science (5–8); Science and technology in local, national, and global challenges (9–12); Science as a human endeavor (K–12); Nature of scientific knowledge (9–12)

- Invite one guest or scientist to your classroom and conduct a television show with a one-to-one interview by taking questions from the "audience." Have students formulate high-quality questions prior to the interview using all levels of Bloom's taxonomy. Submit the show to a local cable channel or to the local education channel for broadcast so that other students have an opportunity to hear the interview and learn about the profession.

WHEN:	During a lesson
CONTENT STANDARD(S):	Science and technology in society (5–8); Nature of science (5–8); Science and technology in local, national, and global challenges (9–12); Science as a human endeavor (K–12); Nature of scientific knowledge (9–12)

- Seek out businesses or community service people who are willing to take on interns. For example, Warren's school had an extremely aggressive and difficult student work on a lobster boat as a part of the school week. Other students have worked at local farms or done video work as interns.

WHEN:	During a lesson
CONTENT STANDARD(S):	Science and technology in local challenges (K–4); Science and technology in society (5–8); Nature of science (5–8); Science and technology in local, national, and global challenges (9–12); Science as a human endeavor (K–12); Nature of scientific knowledge (9–12)

- Engage students in a service-learning project where they are providing a service for their school or community while simultaneously mastering curriculum. For example, have them beautify the school grounds by planning and implementing a butterfly garden. Have them research the necessary components for the garden, perform the essential measurements of the grounds, and calculate what should be planted where, while journaling the entire experience. Service learning is one of the best vehicles for combining interdisciplinary instruction with real-world skills and strategies as well as character.

WHEN:	During a lesson
CONTENT STANDARD(S):	Science and technology in local challenges (K–4); Science and technology in society (5–8); Nature of science (5–8); Science and technology in local, national, and global challenges (9–12); Science as a human endeavor (K–12); Nature of scientific knowledge (9–12)

- For students who participate in the annual Bring Your Child to Work Day, have them debrief with their classmates. Have students research what a debriefing would be like for an astronaut, a scientist making a discovery, an adventurer, and so forth.

WHEN:	During or after a lesson
CONTENT STANDARD(S):	Science and technology in local challenges (K–4); Science and technology in society (5–8); Nature of science (5–8); Science and technology in local, national, and global challenges (9–12); Science as a human endeavor (K–12); Nature of scientific knowledge (9–12)

- Take your students on a field trip to a scientific laboratory or educational outreach program. Since he teaches in Plymouth, Massachusetts, Warren Phillips takes his students to Massachusetts Institute of Technology (MIT) every year where they visit various science laboratories and talk to the scientists about their work. Following the trip, several of the students decide that they would like to be scientists or conduct laboratory work.

WHEN:	After a lesson
CONTENT STANDARD(S):	Science and technology in local challenges (K–4); Science and technology in society (5–8); Nature of science (5–8); Science and technology in local, national, and global challenges (9–12); Science as a human endeavor (K–12); Nature of scientific knowledge (9–12)

- Have students research scientific professions of interest and create reports or projects to share what they have learned with the class. In this way, students get to glean information regarding a variety of occupations for further study.

REFLECTION AND APPLICATION

> How will I incorporate *work study* and *apprenticeships* into instruction to engage students' brains?

Which work study and apprenticeship activities am I already incorporating into my science curriculum?

What additional activities will I incorporate?

Writing and Journals

WHAT: DEFINING THE STRATEGY

A science teacher is lecturing on the states of matter. While listening to the lecture, students are expected to take copious notes. What the teacher doesn't realize is that students' brains can pay conscious attention to only one thing at a time. That doesn't mean that students cannot do more than one thing at a time. After all, there are times when we all have to multitask. What it does mean is that only one thing is in conscious memory, even when performing simultaneous tasks. Therefore, students are either missing part of the lecture while attempting to take many notes or are missing part of the notes while paying attention to the lecture. Well, what is the answer? Why not have students stop periodically during the lecture and take notes in short chunks of information and then continue the lecture. Or prior to the lecture, have them write the notes first. That way the brain has to pay conscious attention to only one thing at a time.

Writing is crucial in that it assists the brain in organizing information and helps with retention. Whatever we write down, we stand a better chance of remembering. Students in science class can help their memory by taking pertinent notes during a lecture, keeping a journal of daily or weekly changes during an experiment, writing up each step in the scientific process as the lab progresses, or reflecting personal feelings related to an assigned service-learning project. Teachers can even stop periodically and ask students to engage in *quick writes.* Two examples would be as follows: (1) Following a lesson on states of matter, have students write the three states; and (2) following a lesson on metric units, have students write the units of the metric system from smallest to largest. Quick writes take only a few seconds, yet they constitute an additional repetition of the information in the brain. When paired with graphic organizers from Strategy 5, a science lecture becomes so much more memorable. Just draw and write on a graphic organizer on the board as you lecture, and have students draw and write along with you. It will make a difference with their comprehension and recall of information!

WHY: THEORETICAL FRAMEWORK

Students need to develop a writing vocabulary, the ability to spell well, the aptitude to organize text, the capacity to think in hierarchies, and the skill to write in a variety of genres including expository and narrative text, business letters, and e-mails. (Fogarty, 2009)

Through journal writing, teachers can focus students' attention on the content, monitor their comprehension of the content, and provide them with opportunities to express their ideas without being embarrassed. (Algozzine, Campbell, & Wang, 2009b)

Writing prompts enable students to extend their thinking to new situations and to show their conceptual understanding and their ability to apply scientific concepts to their personal lives, to technology, or to society as a whole. (Hammerman, 2009)

Students need constant, consistent, and various opportunities to write, to write some more, and to write some more if they are to become skillful with written language. (Fogarty, 2009)

When students create and score rubrics, they are able to focus their writing and think more critically about it. (Algozzine et al., 2009b)

Journals, writer's notebooks, reflections, and diaries take advantage of Gardner's intrapersonal intelligence. (Karten, 2007)

Journal writing assists the brain in making meaning out of the new information it acquires. (Jensen, E., 2004)

Having students do quick writes can be a tool for evaluating how accurate their responses are and can help teachers correct any misunderstandings. (Jensen & Nickelsen, 2008)

It can be distracting to continue talking to students while having them simultaneously write notes or copy notes from the board. (Jensen & Nickelsen, 2008)

When students successfully complete their writing assignments, their explanations help them focus their thoughts and show their basic understanding of a science concept. (Berman, 2008)

During writing, students should be encouraged to describe how content can be applied to their personal lives. (Jensen, E., 2008)

If students are to be skilled as writers, they need multiple and varied chances to practice their craft. (Fogarty, 2009)

If people want to remember an event in detail, they should write down an account of it immediately after it happens. (Markowitz & Jensen, 2007)

Journal writing increases retention and positive transfer of information and can be done at every grade level and in every content area. (Sousa, 2006)

Having students write down what is observed, presented, or thought about helps the brain organize and make sense of extremely complicated and multifaceted bits of information. (Jensen, E., 2001)

HOW: INSTRUCTIONAL ACTIVITIES

WHEN: During a lesson

CONTENT STANDARD(S): Nature of science (5–8), Nature of scientific knowledge (9–12), Science as a human endeavor (K–12), Understanding about scientific inquiry (K–12), Abilities necessary to do scientific inquiry (K–12)

- Instead of giving students a premade notebook (such as a blue book) or a science notebook, have them make their own. An original journal makes it more personal and more valuable to the student. To make them, have students use a half of a piece of oak tag and fold it in half. Then, add plain white or colored paper and fold it in half. Stretch a rubber band over the fold to hold the papers in place. Duplicated sheets can be added to the journal by folding them and placing them under the elastic. Students can sketch their observations or results and provide explanations and labels. Spreadsheets and tables for recording data can be completed and inserted into the journal. Have each student decorate the front cover with graphics, clip art, or drawings about the unit being studied. The back cover can have a map of the local area or ecosystem. Journals containing writings, vocabulary, notes, and drawings from the field can be evaluated with an accompanying rubric and used as a unit grade.

WHEN: During a lesson

CONTENT STANDARD(S): All (K–12)

- When expecting students to take notes or write down meaningful parts of your lecture, provide time for them to do so. Either talk first and then give them time to write, or have them write first and then continue your talk. Otherwise, many students miss out on key points. Pause for younger students to draw pictures rather than write notes.

WHEN:	During a lesson
CONTENT STANDARD(S):	Abilities necessary to do scientific inquiry (K–12); Evidence, models, and explanation (K–12); Understanding about scientific inquiry (K–12)

- Have students write a narrative piece depicting a journey in a time capsule back through the different periods of time (Paleozoic Era, Mesozoic Era, and Cenozoic Era). Students must explain what they saw and heard as they traveled, which forces them to incorporate scientific details about the plant, animal, and geographic features inherent to each era. Younger students can draw pictures depicting each era and explain their pictures rather than write a narrative.

WHEN:	During a lesson
CONTENT STANDARD(S):	Abilities necessary to do scientific inquiry (K–12), Science as a human endeavor (K–12), Understanding about scientific inquiry (K–12)

- As practice, before students write an actual laboratory report, have them write a lab report for making a peanut butter and jelly sandwich. Have them provide a list of materials, procedures or step-by-step instructions, and results. The writer should assume that the reader has no prior knowledge of how to make a sandwich. Younger students can draw the instructions rather than write them. This activity can be much more difficult than it sounds!

WHEN:	During a lesson
CONTENT STANDARD(S):	Systems, order, and organization (5–12); Form and function (5–12); Evidence, models, and explanation (5–12); Abilities necessary to do scientific inquiry (5–12); Understanding about scientific inquiry (5–12)

- Have students write a restaurant review from the point of view of a nutritionist. Have them analyze and compare fats, proteins, and carbohydrates. This assignment can also be done with a nutrition report available at most fast-food establishments.

WHEN:	During a lesson
CONTENT STANDARD(S):	Systems, order, and organization (K–12); Form and function (K–12); Evidence, models, and explanation (K–12); Abilities necessary to do scientific inquiry (K–12); Understanding about scientific inquiry (K–12)

- As you present a *lecturette* (a minilecture of five to seven minutes), stop periodically and have students write phrases or draw key concepts, which will help them remember your important points. Be sure to give them time to write or draw so that their brains will not have to engage in two behaviors simultaneously—listening to your continued talk and trying to remember what to write.

WHEN: During a lesson

CONTENT STANDARD(S): Systems, order, and organization (K–12); Form and function (K–12); Evidence, models, and explanation (K–12); Abilities necessary to do scientific inquiry (K–12); Understanding about scientific inquiry (K–12)

- Incorporate *quick writes* throughout a lesson. Stop periodically during the lesson and have students write a concept just taught. Writing, even for a minute, will help to reinforce the content. For example, stop your lesson and ask students to do the following: *Write the steps in the scientific process.*

WHEN: During or after a lesson

CONTENT STANDARD(S): Systems, order, and organization (K–12); Evidence, models, and explanation (K–12); Understanding about scientific inquiry (K–12)

- Have students make foldable books. Have each student take a topic and create a *hot dog* book, a *step* book, a *pyramid* book, or a *carousel* book. These books are then exchanged between students to help them review or study for a test. There are tutorials and instructions for the bookmaking at www.makingbooks.com.

WHEN: During or after a lesson

CONTENT STANDARD(S): Systems, order, and organization (K–12); Form and function (K–12); Evidence, models, and explanation (K–12); Abilities necessary to do scientific inquiry (K–12); Understanding about scientific inquiry (K–12)

- Have students write narrative or expository selections or draw pictures describing the following:
  o The journey of a bite of food as it travels through the digestive system
  o The journey of a rock traveling with a glacier
  o The journey of the magma in the mantle of the earth as it reaches a volcano

○ The journey of a molecule of oxygen as it enters your body and gets pulled into your lungs

○ The journey of a carbon dioxide molecule as it enters a leaf and travels into its cells

○ The journey of the energy of a sound wave as it creates a sound in a person

○ The journey of a drop of water in the hydrologic cycle

WHEN:	During or after a lesson
CONTENT STANDARD(S):	Systems, order, and organization (K–12); Form and function (K–12); Evidence, models, and explanation (K–12); Abilities necessary to do scientific inquiry (K–12); Understanding about scientific inquiry (K–12)

• Have students write a thank-you note to a system in the human body. Have them thank each part for what they do and explain why it is important to them.

WHEN:	During or after a lesson
CONTENT STANDARD(S):	Systems, order, and organization (5–12); Form and function (5–12); Evidence, models, and explanation (5–12); Abilities necessary to do scientific inquiry (5–12); Understanding about scientific inquiry (5–12)

• Have students pretend that they are journalists who have just witnessed one of the following:

○ A DNA strand replicate and form into two identical chromosomes

○ Mitosis taking place in a cell

○ Photosynthesis

• Have them write a news story that depicts the details of one of the aforementioned processes.

WHEN:	During or after a lesson
CONTENT STANDARD(S):	All (K–12)

• In an effort to improve the quality of the journal writing of students, have them brainstorm an alphabet book that would include vocabulary chunked according to the letters of the alphabet and be pertinent to a unit of study. For example, during a study of content, a science alphabet book might look like the following: amoeba, bacteria, chromosomes, dinosaur, experiment, formula, glacier, and so forth. Post these words as a visual, or have students include them in their notebooks for ready reference.

REFLECTION AND APPLICATION

How will I incorporate *writing* and *journals* into instruction to engage students' brains?

Which writing and journal activities am I already incorporating into my science curriculum?

What additional activities will I incorporate?

Resource

Brain-Compatible Lesson Design

What's next? In other words, how do you incorporate the 20 brain-compatible strategies into your daily science lesson plans? A sample lesson plan can be found at the end of this resource (see Brain-Compatible Science Lesson Plan). Each of the major sections of this plan is described in the paragraphs that follow. It is not necessary that you write or type your plan on the form itself. What is essential is that you ask the following five questions every time you plan a lesson if you want to ensure that it is brain compatible.

An adaptation of this very plan was recently used as teachers and curriculum specialists for the Plymouth, Massachusetts, school district wrote new curricula and sample lesson plans for secondary science content. To see completed lesson plans and handouts from Warren Phillips's classroom, go to www.corwin.com/scienceworksheets.

■ SECTION 1: LESSON OBJECTIVE

What will you be teaching?

The obvious first question when planning a brain-compatible lesson is to consider what you are getting ready to teach. This question is not yours to answer. It is determined by your science content standards and the objectives that naturally flow from those standards. If you attempt to let your textbook determine what you will be teaching, you may not be addressing the knowledge, skills, behaviors, or attitudes that are expected for your grade level or content area. Your science book is only one resource for addressing that knowledge and may not even be the best resource. In addition, if you are using only the textbook, you may feel overwhelmed that you will never cover all of the content. By the way, if all you are doing is *covering* the content, let me paraphrase a renowned educator by the name of Madeline Hunter (2004): *Take a shovel and cover the content with dirt because it is dead to memory as far as the brain is concerned.* Consider this: The textbooks in many school systems around the world are one-third the size of textbooks in the United States and yet many countries outscore our students on tests of academic achievement. Could it be that less is more? Could it be that teachers should examine their curriculum and identify those major concepts that every student needs to know? Could it be that some of those concepts could be chunked, or connected, together and taught simultaneously? In our opening scenarios, both teachers were addressing the Physical Science Content Standard with specific emphasis on *properties and changes of properties in matter.* This is a major chunk of content and should be included in the curriculum for Grades 5 through 8. Now that we know what we are teaching, the remainder of this lesson plan will show us how to make it a brain-compatible, unforgettable lesson.

SECTION 2: ASSESSMENT ■

How will you know students have learned the content?

Waiting until you plan your lesson and then deciding what your students should know and be able to do is actually too late. The research on assessment says, as soon as you know what you will be teaching, the next question becomes, *How will I know students have learned the content I am teaching?*

When I was a student in school, we spent our time trying to guess what the teacher was going to put on the test. If we guessed correctly, we made an A. However, we may have guessed incorrectly and failed, even though we studied. We just studied the wrong thing! Determine what knowledge, skills, behaviors, or attitudes you desire students to have by the end of the lesson and, by all means, tell them! Assessment should not be a well-kept secret. If students know what you expect, they stand a better chance of meeting your expectations. Here's an analogy: If you are an airplane pilot of a private plane, how can you plot your route before you know your destination? You can't! You also cannot plan your lesson before you know your "destination" with students. That is why the assessment question is the second question of the five and not the fifth and last question.

In our sample lesson, students are told at the beginning that by the time they finish the lesson, they should be able to describe in writing in their science journals the properties of solids, liquids, and gases.

SECTION 3: WAYS TO GAIN AND ■
MAINTAIN ATTENTION

How will you gain and maintain students' attention? (Consider need, novelty, meaning, or emotion.)

Here is a bit of bad news! There are so many stimuli in today's environment that the human brain cannot pay attention to everything at once. Therefore, people can be very selective about what they choose to pay attention to. If a teacher's lesson is not worthy of attention, then students' attention is going elsewhere. When the lesson is boring, students are conversing with their peers, peering out the window, paying attention to who is going down the hall, or simply daydreaming. Another bit of bad news! There is a structure in the brain called the hippocampus that helps to determine which parts of what you learn will end up in long-term memory. If your lesson is not deemed important, it stands a slim to none chance of getting past the hippocampus. In fact, the hippocampus will hit the delete key and your lesson will end up in the trash at night. How can you tell if your lesson got deleted? When they come back to class 24 hours later, it is as though they were not present when you were teaching the initial lesson. Has that ever happened to you? It certainly has to me! If you want to grab students' attention, hold it throughout your lesson, and keep your lesson out of the *trash*. There are four ways to do it; they are *need, novelty, meaning,* and *emotion*.

Need

Have you ever learned or remembered something simply because you needed to know it? Need is a big motivator for the brain. For example, years ago I did not see the need to learn how to word process since my secretary typed all of the memos I sent out and anything else I needed her to do. It was not until I began working on my dissertation that I saw the need to learn word processing. After all, Carol couldn't be by my side to type all of the changes I made as I wrote that document, nor could she be at my home late at night or early in the morning when I did most of my writing. I needed to do it myself. So I learned what I needed to know. Now I can word process with the best of them, but I didn't learn it until I saw the need.

Mrs. Miller told students the importance of knowing the properties of each state of matter since everything they come in contact with in the real world is in one of those states. She led a whole-class discussion on the need to know about the various states of matter.

Sometimes, *need* will not work with students. After all, you know that they need specific knowledge or a certain skill, but they do not see the same need. In fact, just telling them that they will need to know the information for a standardized or teacher-made test is not inspiring enough for most students. The good news is that you have three other ways to gain their attention. The second one is novelty.

Novelty

Have you ever noticed that the brain pays attention to things that are new or different in the environment? Things to which we become accustomed become mundane and require little special attention. I related this story in another one of my books, but it bears repeating. I fly three to five times a week most weeks and have heard the flight instructions given by the flight attendant so many times that I could actually get up and tell the passengers myself. I can even physically show you where the exits are. So when the instructions are being given, I am usually reading a book. During the several times that I have flown Southwest Airlines, I have noticed that they give the instructions in novel ways. One time they were singing them to the theme song for the *Beverly Hillbillies*. Another time, they were giving the instructions in rap; and a third time, the flight attendant was using humor. Each and every time I listened intently because of the novelty involved. They had my attention!

There are only 20 strategies on the list. Where is the novelty in that? Well, think about it. Every one of those 20 strategies has inherent in it endless possibilities for novelty. Think of all the different stories you can tell, or the music you can incorporate, or even the projects in which you can engage your students. The possibilities are endless!

In the sample lesson, Mrs. Miller uses a number of the 20 strategies at some point during the lesson to teach students about the properties of matter. They will be delineated as we answer question five.

Meaning

Students have often been heard asking this question, *Why do we have to learn this?* This question indicates that students see no relevance in what is being taught and how it applies to their personal lives. For content to be meaningful, it needs to be connected in some way to students' lives. For example, I observed a teacher's lesson involving communicable diseases. To make the lesson more meaningful, she placed specks of glitter on the hands of one student in class and asked him to move about the room. By the time he had finished, most of the students in the class had at least one or two specks of glitter on them resulting from contact directly from the original student or from another student who had come in contact with the original student. This activity helped the class see just how quickly and easily disease and illness can be spread among humans.

In the sample lesson, Mrs. Miller had students find objects at home that represented the different states of matter. This connection to real life made the lesson much more meaningful.

Emotion

Of all four ways to gain the brain's attention, emotion is probably the most powerful. Why? Emotion places information in one of the strongest memory systems in the brain, reflexive memory. Anything that happened in the world that was emotional, you will not soon forget where you were when it happened.

Yet teachers do not want to engage students in negative emotional experiences that are not good for learning. While they will not forget the experience, they will not remember the content acquired during the experience. For example, when I am reading on the plane, as long as the flight is smooth and there is light to moderate turbulence, I can concentrate on the text and comprehend what I am reading. However, several times I have been on flights where we encountered extreme turbulence. All of a sudden, even if I pretend to be calm and reading, I am reading the same paragraph over and over, and if questioned, would not remember one thing that I supposedly read. The ride has become too emotional. My definition of an emotional teacher is one who teaches with emotion and passion.

Mrs. Miller loves science and her passion rubs off on her students, so much so that several parents report that their children are excited about science for the first time in their educational careers. In the sample lesson, several of the activities provide excitement and an enthusiasm for the topic.

A teacher does not need to feel compelled to include all four ways to get a student's attention: need, novelty, meaning, and emotion. If they can effectively incorporate one, it can lead to a great lesson.

■ **SECTION 4: CONTENT CHUNKS**

How will you divide and teach the content to engage students' brains?

Join me in an activity that will help to prove that the brain thinks in connections. Try this with students or even with members of your family. Ask them to spell the word *coast* three times (c-o-a-s-t, c-o-a-s-t, c-o-a-s-t). Then, quickly ask them, *What do you put in a toaster?* Nine times out of ten, the answer will be *toast,* when the correct answer is *bread.* The brain connected or associated the word *coast* with the rhyming word *toast.* When you connect content together, remember that even the adult brain can hold only between five and nine, or an average of seven, isolated facts in short-term memory simultaneously. This is why so much in life comes in a series of sevens. For example, there are seven days in a week, numbers in a phone number, notes on the scale, colors in the rainbow, seas, continents, habits of highly effective people, initial multiple intelligences, or even dwarfs.

If adults are expected to hold more than seven items, then the content needs to be chunked, or connected. This is why a social security number, a telephone number, or a credit card number is in chunks, to make it easier for them to remember. The brain considers a chunk as one thing, rather than separate things. Therefore, look at your curriculum and identify those major chunks that every student needs to know in science this year. Remember to include at least one activity in each chunk. It is the activity that enables the brain to process the chunk! Your students will thank you for it!

In the sample lesson, Mrs. Miller was able to teach all the states of matter as one concept, or one chunk. However, a number of activities were used to enable students to process the chunk. By the way, all of the activities in a chunk do not need to be experienced in one lesson, or one day. The lesson plan may span several days or longer.

■ **SECTION 5: BRAIN-COMPATIBLE STRATEGIES**

Which will you use to deliver content?

All 20 of the brain-compatible strategies are listed at the bottom of the lesson plan. In this way, you will not have to remember them because you have them listed for ready reference. Even I can't always remember the 20 strategies when I need to do so! As you are determining what activities you will include in each chunk of your lesson, you should be incorporating some of the 20 brain-compatible strategies. If you get to the end of your plan and you cannot check off any of the strategies (possibly because your entire lesson consisted of long lectures or worksheets, neither of which is brain compatible), go back and plan your lesson again. It will not meet the needs of the majority of your students and may not even be recalled after a 24-hour period.

I have often been asked this question, *How many strategies should I incorporate in one lesson, or one chunk?* There is no magic number. Using too many strategies at one time can be just as detrimental as using too few. A rule of thumb I try to teach by is as follows: Make sure that at some point during the lesson, you have incorporated at least one visual, one auditory, one tactile, and one kinesthetic strategy since you will have students with all four different preferences in your classroom. That doesn't mean one strategy of each modality per chunk, but one strategy of each modality per objective.

Keep this in mind: If you use one strategy, say, music, to teach a lesson and the entire class grasps the concept, then by all means, move on to the next concept. You taught it and they got it! However, if you use one strategy, say, music, to teach a lesson and part of the class understands the concept and the other part does not, use a different strategy from a different modality for the reteaching. Simply doing the same thing again and louder has never worked!

By the time the lesson in our good scenario was completed, students had experienced at least the following seven strategies: music, discussion, role play, movement, drawing, visuals, and graphic organizers. They had sung "The States of Matter" and participated in a class discussion (auditory), they had physically simulated the movement of molecules with their hands and with their bodies (kinesthetic), they had drawn molecules for all the states of matter (tactile), and they had seen and drawn a graphic organizer describing the states (visual and tactile).

SUMMARY ■

Well, we've come to the end of another book. My hope is that I have accomplished what I set out to do, which was as follows:

- Introduce you to 20 strategies that take advantage of ways in which the brain learns best
- Supply over 200 research rationales from experts in the field as to why these strategies work better than others
- Provide more than 250 activities of how to incorporate the 20 strategies into a K–12 science classroom
- Correlate the science content standards to each activity
- Allow time and space at the end of each chapter for the reader to reflect on the application of the strategies as they apply directly to the reader's specific objectives
- Ask and answer the five questions that every teacher ought to be asking when planning and teaching a brain-compatible science lesson

Of all the content areas, science probably lends itself best to the highly engaging, brain-compatible way of delivering content. Take those major science concepts or chunks you will be teaching this year and incorporate those strategies that will not only increase student achievement but also get them so turned on to science that many may decide to make science their life's work!

BRAIN-COMPATIBLE SCIENCE LESSON PLAN

Lesson Objective(s): *What will you be teaching?*

_____

Assessment (Traditional/Authentic): *How will you know students have learned the content?*

_____

Ways to Gain/Maintain Attention (Primacy): *How will you gain and maintain students' attention? Consider need, novelty, meaning, or emotion.*

_____

Content Chunks: *How will you divide and teach the content to engage students' brains?*

Lesson Segment 1:

Activities:

Lesson Segment 2:

Activities:

Lesson Segment 3:

Activities:

_____

Brain-Compatible Strategies: *Which will you use to deliver content?*

☐ Brainstorming/Discussion
☐ Drawing/Artwork
☐ Field Trips
☐ Games
☐ Graphic Organizers/Semantic Maps/Word Webs
☐ Humor
☐ Manipulatives/Experiments/Labs/Models
☐ Metaphors/Analogies/Similes
☐ Mnemonic Devices
☐ Movement
☐ Music/Rhythm/Rhyme/Rap

☐ Project-/Problem-Based Instruction
☐ Reciprocal Teaching/Cooperative Learning
☐ Role Plays/Drama/Pantomimes/Charades
☐ Storytelling
☐ Technology
☐ Visualization/Guided Imagery
☐ Visuals
☐ Work Study/Apprenticeships
☐ Writing/Journals

Bibliography

Algozzine, B., Campbell, P., & Wang, A. (2009a). *63 Tactics for teaching diverse learners: Grades K–6.* Thousand Oaks, CA: Corwin.

Algozzine, B., Campbell, P., & Wang, A. (2009b). *63 Tactics for teaching diverse learners: Grades 6–12.* Thousand Oaks, CA: Corwin.

Allen, R. (2008a). *Green light classrooms: Teaching techniques that accelerate learning.* Victoria, Australia: Hawker Brownlow.

Allen, R. (2008b). *The ultimate book of music for learning.* Victoria, Australia: Hawker Brownlow.

Angelo, T., & Cross, K. P. (1993). *Classroom assessment techniques: A handbook for college teachers.* San Francisco: Jossey-Bass.

Barr, R. D., & Parrett, W. (2007). *Saving our students, saving our schools: 50 Proven strategies for helping.* Thousand Oaks, CA: Corwin.

Bell, A. (2005). *Creating digital video in your school: How to shoot, edit, produce, distribute, and incorporate digital media into curriculum.* Worthington, OH: Linworth.

Berman, S. (2008). *Thinking strategies for science: Grades 5–12* (2nd ed.). Victoria, Australia: Hawker Brownlow.

Berns, B. B., & Sandler, J. O. (Eds.). (2009). *Making science curriculum matter: Wisdom for the reform road ahead.* Thousand Oaks, CA: Corwin & Education Development Center.

Berryman, S. E., & Bailey, T. R. (1992). *The double helix of education and the economy.* New York: Institute on Education and the Economy, Columbia University Teachers College.

Breaux, A., & Whitaker, T. (2006). *Seven simple secrets: What the best teachers know and do.* Larchmont, NY: Eye On Education.

Brooks, J. (2002). *Schooling for life.* Alexandria, VA: Association for Supervision and Curriculum Development.

Caine, G., & Caine, R. (2006). *Making connections: Teaching & the human brain* (3rd ed.). Thousand Oaks, CA: Corwin.

Caine, R. N., & Caine, G. (1994). *Making connections: Teaching and the human brain.* Menlo Park, CA: Addison-Wesley.

Caine, R. N., Caine, G., McClintic, C., & Klimek, K. (2005). *12 Brain/mind learning principles in action: The fieldbook for making connections, teaching, and the human brain.* Thousand Oaks, CA: Corwin.

Caine, R. N., Caine, G., McClintic, C., & Klimek, K. J. (2009). *12 Brain/mind learning principles in action: Developing executive functions of the human brain.* Thousand Oaks, CA: Corwin.

California Department of Education. (n.d.). *Exploratorium snacks.* Available from www.exploratorium.edu/snacks

Costa, A. L. (2008). *The school as a home for the mind: Creating mindful curriculum, instruction, and dialogue* (2nd ed.). Victoria, Australia: Hawker Brownlow.

Damasio, A. (1999). *The feeling of what happens.* New York: Harcourt.

Daniels, H., & Zemelman, S. (2004). *Subjects matter: Every teacher's guide to content-area reading.* Portsmouth, NH: Heinemann.

Davis, L. (2002). *The importance of field trips.* Retrieved from http://gsa.confex .com.gsa/2002RM/finalprogram/abstract_33868.htm

Dewey, J. (1934). *Art as experience.* New York: Minton Balch.

Dewey, J. (1938). *Experience and education.* New York: Macmillan.

Eggspert® is a registered trademark of Educational Insights, Inc.

E-Pals Global Community. (2010). Retrieved from www.epals.com

Faryadi, Q. (2007). *Enlightening advantages of cooperative learning.* Retrieved from ERIC database. (ED495702)

Feinstein, S. (2009). *Secrets of the teenage brain: Research-based strategies for reaching and teaching today's adolescents* (2nd ed.). Thousand Oaks, CA: Corwin.

Fogarty, R. (1997). *Brain-compatible classrooms.* Thousand Oaks, CA: Corwin.

Fogarty, R. (2001). *Making sense of the research on the brain and learning.* Victoria, Australia: Hawker Brownlow.

Fogarty, R. (2009). *Brain-compatible classrooms* (3rd ed.). Victoria, Australia: Hawker Brownlow.

Gardner, H. (1983). *Frames of mind: The theory of multiple intelligences.* New York: Basic Books.

Gettinger, M., & Kohler, K. M. (2006). Process-outcome approaches to classroom management and effective teaching. In C. Evertson, C. M. Weinstein, & C. S. Weinstein (Eds.), *Handbook of classroom management: Research, practice, and contemporary issues* (pp. 73–95). Mahwah, NJ: Erlbaum.

Glasser, W. (1999). *Choice theory: A new psychology of personal freedom.* New York: HarperCollins.

Goldberg, C. (2004). Brain friendly techniques: Mind mapping. *School Library Media Activities Monthly, 21*(3), 22–24.

Gregory, G., & Chapman, C. (2002). *Differentiated instruction: One size doesn't fit all.* Thousand Oaks, CA: Corwin.

Gregory, G. H., & Parry, T. (2006). *Designing brain-compatible learning* (3rd ed.). Thousand Oaks, CA: Corwin.

Hammerman, E. (2009). *Formative assessment strategies for enhanced learning in science, K–8.* Thousand Oaks, CA: Corwin.

Hiraoka, L. (2006, March). All this talk about tech. *NEA Today, 24,* 6.

Hunter, R. (2004). *Madeline Hunter's mastery teaching: Increasing instructional effectiveness in elementary and secondary schools.* Thousand Oaks, CA: Corwin.

HyperStudio® is a product of The Software MacKiev Company.

Institute for the Advancement of Research in Education. (2003). *Graphic organizers: A review of scientifically based research.* Portland, OR: Inspiration Software. Available from www.inspiration.com

IMAX® is a registered trademark of IMAX Corporation.

iPod® is a registered trademark of Apple Computer, Inc.

iTunes® is a registered trademark of Apple Computer, Inc.

Jensen, E. (2001). *Arts with the brain in mind.* Alexandria, VA: Association for Supervision and Curriculum Development.

Jensen, E. (2004). *Brain-compatible strategies* (2nd ed.). Thousand Oaks, CA: Corwin.

Jensen, E. (2005). *Top tunes for teaching: 977 Song titles and practical tools for choosing the right music every time.* Thousand Oaks, CA: Corwin.

Jensen, E. (2008). *Brain-based learning: The new paradigm of teaching* (2nd ed.). Thousand Oaks, CA: Corwin.

Jensen, E. (2009). *Super teaching* (4th ed.). Thousand Oaks, CA: Corwin.

Jensen, E., & Dabney, M. (2000). *Learning smarter: The new science of teaching.* San Diego, CA: The Brain Store.

Jensen, E., & Nickelsen, L. (2008). *Deeper learning: 7 Powerful strategies for in-depth and longer-lasting learning.* Thousand Oaks, CA: Corwin.

Jensen, R. (2008). *Catalyst teaching: High-impact teaching techniques for the science classroom.* Victoria, Australia: Hawker Brownlow.

Jones, C. (2008). *The magic of metaphor.* Retrieved from www.Uxmatters.com/mt/archives/2008/php

Kagan, S., & Kagan, M. (2007). *Multiple intelligences: The complete MI book.* Victoria, Australia: Hawker Brownlow.

Karten, T. J. (2007). *More inclusion strategies that work!* Victoria, Australia: Hawker Brownlow.

Karten, T. J. (2009). *Inclusion strategies that work for adolescent learners.* Thousand Oaks, CA: Corwin.

Keeley, P. (2008). *Science formative assessment: 75 Practical strategies for linking assessment, instruction, and learning.* Thousand Oaks, CA: Corwin & National Science Teachers Association.

Koosh® is a registered trademark of Oddzon, Inc.

Krepel, W. J., & Duvall, C. R. (1981). *Field trips: A guide for planning and conducting educational experiences.* Washington, DC: National Education Association.

Kuhlmann, S., Kirschbaum, C., & Wolf, O. T. (2005). Effects of oral cortisol treatment in healthy young women on memory retrieval of negative and neutral words. *Neurobiology of Learning and Memory, 83,* 158–162.

LeBoutillier, N., & Marks, D. F. (2003). Mental imagery and creativity: A meta-analytic review study. *British Journal of Psychology, 94,* 29–44.

Lakoff, G., & Johnson, M. (1980). *Metaphors we live by.* Chicago: University of Chicago Press.

Mangan, M. A. (2007). *Brain-compatible science* (2nd ed.). Thousand Oaks, CA: Corwin.

Markowitz, K., & Jensen, E. (1999). *The great memory book.* Thousand Oaks, CA: Corwin.

Markowitz, K., & Jensen, E. (2007). *The great memory book.* Victoria, Australia: Hawker Brownlow.

Marzano, R. J. (2007). *The art and science of teaching: A comprehensive framework for effective instruction.* Victoria, Australia: Hawker Brownlow.

Mayer, R. E. (2003). *Learning and instruction.* Upper Saddle River, NJ: Prentice Hall.

McCormick Tribune Foundation. (1999). *Ten things every child needs* [DVD]. Chicago: Chicago Production Center.

Mentos® is a registered trademark of Perfetti Van Melle.

Microsoft. (2005). Photo Story (Version 3) [Software]. Available from www.microsoft.com/windowsxp/using/digitalphotography/photostory/default.mspx

National Research Council. (1996). *National Science Education Standards.* Washington, DC: National Academies Press. Available from www.nap.edu/openbook.php?record_id=4962

National Geographic. (n.d.). *The Jason project.* Available from www.jason.org/public/whatis/start.aspx

National Research Council of the National Academies. (2006). *America's lab report: Investigations in high school science.* Washington, DC: National Academy Press.

National Science Teachers Association. (2006). Picturing to learn makes science visual. *NSTA Reports, 18*(2), 20.

Nerf ball® is a registered trademark of Hasbro, Inc.

Nevills, P., & Wolfe, P. (2009). *Building the reading brain: PreK–3* (2nd ed.). Thousand Oaks, CA: Corwin.

Ogle, D. M. (2000). Make it visual: A picture is worth a thousand words. In M. McLaughlin & M. Vogt (Eds.), *Creativity and innovation in content area teaching.* Norwood, MA: Christopher-Gordon.

Paulin, M. G. (2005). Evolutionary origins and principles of distributed neural computation for state estimation and movement control in vertebrates. *Complexity, 10*(3), 56–65.

Pereira, A. C., Huddleston, D. E., Brickman, A. M., Sosunov, A. A., Hen, R., McKhann, G. M., et al. (2007). An in vivo correlate of exercise-induced neurogenesis in the adult dentate gyrus. *Proceedings of the National Academy of Sciences, USA, 104,* 5638–5643.

Photo Story 3 is a product of Microsoft Corporation.

Pinkerton, K. (1994). Using brain-based techniques in high school science. *Teaching and Change, 2*(1), 44–61.

Popsicle® is a registered trademark of Unilever Supply Chain, Inc.

Posamentier, A. S., & Jaye, D. (2006). *What successful math teachers do, Grades 6–12: 79 Research-based strategies for the standards-based classroom.* Thousand Oaks, CA: Corwin.

Pringles® is a registered trademark of Procter & Gamble Company.

Quizzillion® is a registered trademark of Learning Resources, Inc.

Ronis, D. L. (2006). *Brain-compatible mathematics* (2nd ed.). Thousand Oaks, CA: Corwin.

Sebesta, L. M., & Martin, S. R. M. (2004). Fractions: Building a foundation with concrete manipulatives. *Illinois Schools Journal, 83*(2), 3–23.

Sheffield, C. (2007). Technology and the gifted adolescent: Higher order thinking, 21st century literacy, and the digital native. *Meridian: A Middle School Computer Technologies Journal, 10*(2). Retrieved from www.ncsu.edu/meridian/sum 2007/gifted/index.htm

Silverstein, S. (1964). *The giving tree.* New York: HarperCollins.

Slinky® is a registered trademark of POOF-Slinky, Inc.

Society for Developmental Education. (1995). *Pyramid of learning.* Peterborough, NH: Author.

Sousa, D. A. (2006). *How the brain learns* (3rd ed.). Thousand Oaks, CA: Corwin.

Sprenger, M. (2007). *Memory 101 for educators.* Thousand Oaks, CA: Corwin.

Sternberg, R. J., & Grigorenko, E. L. (2000). *Teaching for successful intelligence: To increase student learning and achievement.* Arlington Heights, IL: Skylight.

Sylwester, R. (2003). *A biological brain in a cultural classroom* (2nd ed.). Thousand Oaks, CA: Corwin.

Tate, M. (2007). *Shouting won't grow dendrites: 20 Techniques for managing a brain-compatible classroom.* Thousand Oaks, CA: Corwin.

Tate, M. (2010). *Worksheets don't grow dendrites: 20 Instructional strategies that engage the brain* (2nd ed.). Thousand Oaks, CA: Corwin.

Teflon® is a registered trademark of E. I. du Pont de Nemours and Company.

Udvari-Solner, A., & Kluth, P. (2008). *Joyful learning: Active and collaborative learning in inclusive classrooms.* Thousand Oaks, CA: Corwin.

Time Magazine. Friday, August 1, 1969. Environment: The cities: The price of optimism. Retrieved September 23, 2010, from www.time.com/time/magazine/article/0,9171,901182-1,00.html

Underwood, J. (2009). *Today, I made a difference.* Avon, MA: Adams Media.

Weinberger, N. M. (2004). Music and the brain. *Scientific American, 291*(5), 88–95.

Westwater, A., & Wolfe, P. (2000, November). The brain-compatible curriculum. *Educational Leadership, 58*(3), 49–52.

Wiggins, G., & McTighe, J. (2008, May). Put understanding first. *Educational Leadership, 65*(19), 36–41.

Wilhelm, J. (1997). *You gotta BE the book: Teaching engaged and reflective reading with adolescents.* New York: Teachers College Press.

Wonacott, M. E. (1993). *Apprenticeship and the future of the work force.* ERIC Digest No. 124. Retrieved August 19, 2010, from www.ericdigests.org/1992-3/future.htm

Yager, R. (Ed.). (2006). *Exemplary science in Grades 5–8: Standards-based success stories.* Arlington, VA: National Science Teachers Association.

Zull, J. (2004, September). The art of changing the brain. *Educational Leadership, 62*(1), 68–72.

Index

CORWIN

A SAGE Company

The Corwin logo—a raven striding across an open book—represents the union of courage and learning. Corwin is committed to improving education for all learners by publishing books and other professional development resources for those serving the field of PreK–12 education. By providing practical, hands-on materials, Corwin continues to carry out the promise of its motto: **"Helping Educators Do Their Work Better."**